"In this epic season of revival, God is opening [...] phetic dreams are breaking out like never be[...] another timely book that will help you to pa[...] *Awaken the Dreamscape* imparts keys to recog[...] and to encounter more of God as you do so. I believe your faith will go to another level as you read this book!"

Dr. Ché Ahn, senior leader, Harvest Rock Church, Pasadena, California; president, Harvest International Ministry; international chancellor, Wagner University

"Jennifer Eivaz has given us an incredibly anointed and revelatory handbook on understanding and interpreting our dreams. She expertly walks us through a biblically sound, in-depth study of heavenly dreams. Dreams are the least understood and most unappreciated gift God has given His children, and Jennifer has advanced understanding and powerful authority to help God's people experience the full promise of this amazing blessing. It is time for you to dream dreams, and this book is your guide to the greatest adventure God has for you!"

Dr. Michael Maiden, senior pastor, Church for the Nations; author, *What is Heaven Saying?*

"God is communicating to us ALL the time, and sometimes even when we are asleep! Dreams are a beautiful way that the Lord speaks to us often through prophetic symbolization, warnings, insights, and promises. When you dream, it's like God hands you a treasure map, and treasure maps often need an interpretation to understand and follow the steps towards the destiny. My friend Jennifer Eivaz has written a most beautiful book that gives wonderful guidelines for navigating your prophetic dreams. Even the appendix alone is amazingly insightful! Get ready to unlock understanding for what God is trying to speak to you!"

Ana Werner, seer prophet; founder, president, Eagles Network; author, *The Seer's Path*

"Metaphors, symbols, images, sounds, and colors are replete in heaven's primary language—dreams! In fact, dreams are a 'last days' language of God. While everyone dreams, few can interpret and understand. This is why *Awaken the Dreamscape* is a powerful gift and tool. Through Jennifer's personal God-dreams, encounters, and supernatural experiences, she presents a fresh new perspective on this subject, which is oftentimes mysterious, ethereal, or perhaps even spooky. She shares powerful principles and practical tools on how to understand and interpret dreams tethered to the Word of God while activating the dreamer inside of you. I highly recommend this book."

Tony Kim, vice president, Harvest International Ministry; founder, ROAR Reformation Movement; pastor, Renaissance Church

"Our good friend Jennifer Eivaz has penned another literary masterpiece. Rarely does someone have divine insight into areas of visions, dreams, and supernatural ministry, so much so that when you read their books, you say, 'Wow, I've been there, and I've experienced that' or 'Now I have language to place with what I've been going through,' which is exactly what happens when you read one of Jennifer's books. Each of her books provides a solution to a problem on the earth. When you finish a book, you walk away more empowered and enlightened than before. Whenever she writes, it's from a place of firsthand experiential knowledge.

In *Awaken the Dreamscape*, Jennifer shares wisdom about visions and dreams and how they tie in to and unlock the supernatural realm in common language. She helps us to navigate through the various parts and images revealed in dreams and explains each of them in language that we can understand.

As you read through these pages you will find that Jennifer equips you with the knowledge you will need to navigate and interpret your visions and dreams."

LaJun and Valora Cole, lead servants, Contagious Church Tampa, Florida; founders, LaJun & Valora Cole Ministries; authors, *Divine Dispatch*

"Jennifer Eivaz is a prophet, minister, and leader of the highest caliber, character, and maturity. Her keen and road-tested wisdom is second to none. If you have read any of her revelatory books, you will already know that in reading *Awaken the Dreamscape* you are going to be inspired, challenged, well-equipped, and you will gain great insight. This is one of those books that you will want to keep near as you will find yourself referring to it again and again.

We consider it a great honor to recommend and endorse to you both our dear friend Jennifer Eivaz and her powerful book *Awaken the Dreamscape*."

Ben and Jodie Hughes, founders, Pour It Out Ministries

"Understanding the dream realm is vital for our spiritual growth and life. One God dream interpreted the correct way can change the course of your life. Jennifer's book will give the reader fresh revelation and be a tool around the world to those who grab hold of it. We spend a large portion of our life sleeping, and God uses that time to talk to us about our past, present, and future. This book will be a significant guide to unravel truth and dismantle doubt or confusion concerning your dream life. I want to personally recommend this book to those who are in search of answers for their dreams."

Apostle John Eckhardt, author, *Prayers That Rout Demons*; founder, Impact University

"*Awaken the Dreamscape* is to dreams as Jennifer Eivaz's *Inner Healing and Deliverance Handbook* is to deliverance ministry—incredibly insightful and full of godly wisdom. The market is saturated with secular and occultic dream interpretation books, guides, and manuals. The Kingdom has suffered due to lack of teaching in this area. You will find this book to be a valuable resource as you navigate the dream world. Thank you, Jennifer, for giving us exactly what we have been in need of."

John Bates, John Bates Ministries; author, *Inner Hearing* and *You Are What You Eat*; entrepreneur; inventor

Awaken
the
DREAMSCAPE

Books by Jennifer Eivaz

The Intercessors Handbook
Seeing the Supernatural
Glory Carriers
Prophetic Secrets
Inner Healing and Deliverance Handbook
Awaken the Dreamscape

Awaken

the

DREAMSCAPE

THE BUILDING BLOCKS FOR UNDERSTANDING THE SUPERNATURAL POWER OF YOUR DREAMS

Jennifer Eivaz

Chosen

a division of Baker Publishing Group
Minneapolis, Minnesota

© 2024 by Jennifer Eivaz

Published by Chosen Books
Minneapolis, Minnesota
www.chosenbooks.com

Chosen Books is a division of
Baker Publishing Group, Grand Rapids, Michigan
Printed in the United States of America

Library of Congress Cataloging-in-Publication Data
Names: Eivaz, Jennifer, author.
Title: Awaken the dreamscape : the building blocks for understanding the supernatural power of your dreams / Jennifer Eivaz.
Description: Minneapolis, Minnesota : Chosen Books, a division of Baker Publishing Group, [2024] | Includes bibliographical references.
Identifiers: LCCN 2023032724 | ISBN 9780800762148 (paper) | ISBN 9780800772673 (casebound) | ISBN 9781493445080 (ebook)
Subjects: LCSH: Dreams—Religious aspects—Christianity. | Dream interpretation.
Classification: LCC BR115.D74 E35 2024 | DDC 248.2/9—dc23/eng/20230906
LC record available at https://lccn.loc.gov/2023032724

24 25 26 27 28 29 30   7 6 5 4 3 2 1

I dedicate this book to my friend, the Holy Spirit,
who has always given me eyes to see and understanding
into the realms of dreams and visions.

Contents

Foreword

Katherine Ruonala

It is with great pleasure and excitement that I introduce to you my dear friend Jennifer Eivaz's new book, *Awaken the Dreamscape*. Within its pages, you will embark on a remarkable journey into the mysterious realm of dream interpretation, discovering a wealth of wisdom and guidance on how to navigate the dreams that grace your nights.

I have experienced the profound impact of dreams as a means through which the Lord speaks to me regularly. As I have learned to seek the Holy Spirit, the Revealer of mysteries, for understanding, I have been wonderfully led and prepared by the Lord to discern how to pray and respond to various situations. Now I often ask the Holy Spirit to help me understand even the dreams I once dismissed as insignificant, for I have come to realize that the Holy Spirit often reveals hidden truths and insights through them.

I remember once having a dream where I had a cut on my leg and my father (who in the natural is a doctor) looked at it and said it was "Singapore polio" (polio being a disease that can hinder your ability to walk or run), and then I woke up. Ordinarily I would have put this dream down to being too hot under the covers, but as I had started to understand that God often wants to speak to me through my dreams, I took it to the Lord in my prayer time. Immediately, the Holy Spirit began to interpret it for me. He showed me that the cut on my leg was an offense I had against someone, and that God (the doctor) wanted to heal it so that it didn't negatively affect my call to international ministry. (Singapore represented to me the gateway to the nations from Australia.) Then I had a wonderful encounter with the Lord as I asked Him to forgive me for holding unforgiveness and offense, and He healed my heart. I would have missed that wonderful encounter with the Lord had I not taken time to bring my dream to the Holy Spirit for interpretation. Dreams are indeed one of the powerful ways through which God desires to communicate with us, and *Awaken the Dreamscape* shows you how to bring your dreams before the Lord and offers valuable tools to unlock their messages.

Jennifer Eivaz's book provides wise and biblical guidance for unraveling the symbolism and hidden meanings within your dreams. With her pastoral and prophetic experience, Jennifer offers invaluable insights that will equip you to embark on a transformative journey with the Holy Spirit.

Having had the privilege of reading this captivating work, I can confidently say that *Awaken the Dreamscape* is a greatly needed book. Its practical and wise advice will truly help individuals mature in this prophetic dimension. The pages overflow with invaluable knowledge and wise counsel, ensuring that you can fully embrace the divine messages delivered through your dreams.

Jennifer's personal stories will encourage and inspire you to understand and embrace the dreamscape. Each chapter is infused with wisdom and a genuine desire to empower readers on their spiritual journeys. Jennifer's passion for dream interpretation shines through, making this book not only a captivating read but also an indispensable resource you will want to refer to again and again.

Dear readers, I wholeheartedly invite you to immerse yourself in the world of *Awaken the Dreamscape* and embark on a transformative adventure. By the power of the Holy Spirit and through the biblically sound wisdom and guidance within these pages, I pray that you will unlock the full potential of your dreams and awaken a deeper understanding of what the Lord desires to say to you.

May this book inspire you to pay closer attention to the divine messages concealed within your dreams. Enjoy the exploration of the dreamscape ahead, and may your journey be filled with spiritual growth and revelation.

With love,

Katherine Ruonala
Senior leader of Glory City Church Brisbane; founder and facilitator of the Australian Prophetic Council; author of *Living in the Miraculous, From Wilderness to Wonders, Life with the Holy Spirit, Supernatural Freedom, Speak Life,* and *Double for Your Trouble*

Acknowledgments

I want to thank my wonderful husband, Ron Eivaz, and my children, David and Christiana, for their love, prayers, and endless support as I took time away from them to finish this book. They've made sacrifices for several years to accommodate my writing schedule and have done so without complaint. I am so grateful for my family and their consistent efforts to make room for more and more books to come through my life.

I also want to thank the staff and congregants at Harvest Church (Turlock, California) for their love and consistent support. They've always championed me as an author and speaker and given me plenty of room to deposit these books around the globe. I am truly blessed and honored to be co-pastoring some of the best people in the world.

Thank you, Chantal and Dottie, for your patience, friendship, encouragement, and powerful intercession as I wrestled to bring this book to life.

Thank you, Pastor Elaina and Pastor Alex, for your support and patience and for fully covering the needs of the church while I was absent to work out the pages of this book.

My heartfelt thanks to Pastors Brad and Lisa Joss of Paradox Church in western Australia for their continual partnership and friendship. I've partially written four of my books on their beach shores as this area of the world is definitely a nest for rest. *Awaken the Dreamscape* was actually birthed and finished in western Australia. I didn't plan to do that, but that's how it worked out, and I don't think it was a coincidence. By the way, *Awaken the Dreamscape* has reminded me so much of what I experienced with my second book, *Seeing the Supernatural*. I felt as if I were working hard throughout to create plain language for deep spiritual realities, truths I've known internally but never put to paper for others to read and run with. I've also experienced a felt spiritual encounter throughout the writing process, along with strangely similar spiritual warfare. For these reasons, I'm looking forward to seeing what the Holy Spirit does with this book, knowing it will shape and transform the spiritual landscape of many people's lives.

Finally, I want to thank the Holy Spirit for His precious encounter that happened within just hours of finishing this book. I have no words to describe what took place, but I am left in holy awe.

Introduction

HE FIGHTS FOR YOU

The foundation was set for this book when I discovered that a unique realm for visions and dreams seemed to overshadow parts or most of Australia. That sounds like a big, overarching statement right there. I'll explain what I mean, only I'll first need to provide the backstory. In my book *Glory Carriers*, I wrote in detail about the spiritual warfare I endured my first time heading into this nation.[1] The short story is that I began to battle with an ancient snake-like deity highly venerated by Australia's indigenous population. It's commonly known as the Rainbow Serpent and hosts a hybrid of attributes, such as the traditional Leviathan spirit (the demonic king of pride)[2] and a python spirit, which is a spirit of divination.[3] I came to this conclusion based on the clear and undeniable outflow of warfare that I encountered from the onset, which was then confirmed by repeating themes of deliverance that consistently came up with people when I ministered there.

The spiritual attack came in the form of a mysterious respiratory illness just a few weeks before I went to western Australia to conduct a prayer conference. I could hardly breathe, which earned me an unexpected trip to the emergency room followed by five days of bed rest. I'm one of those people who never stops moving, so five days in bed was a big deal. While resting, I began to research the area and noticed the impact of this deity on the entire land. You can trace elements of it almost everywhere, including the art, roadways, waterways, and in the overall architecture.

The apostle Paul provides a description of this kind of spiritual battle. He wrote, "For we do not wrestle against flesh and blood, but against principalities, against powers, against the rulers of the darkness of this age, against spiritual hosts of wickedness in the heavenly places" (Ephesians 6:12).

This ancient deity was definitely a key spiritual stronghold in Australia, and it was now buffeting me. Think about what a python does to its prey in the natural, and you'll understand why my breathing was arrested right before I entered the land. I was in a wrestling match for sure, not yet realizing the treasure on the other side of this battle.

I would probably have to be Indigenous Australian in order to fully comprehend what they affirm as their creation story and subsequent culture formation. Although there are variations of the story among the five hundred different tribes and just as many dialects, generally speaking, they believe land creation was, in part, the result of this particular serpent spirit and centered around something called the Dreamtime, or Dreaming, which was a beginning that never ended and remains a continuum of past, present, and future.[4] In other words, it's a realm where time does not exist. One western Australian tribe believes that the snake-like dreaming creature (which they call Wagyl) is responsible for making rivers, waterways, and other landforms they consider sacred.

According to 1 Samuel 9:9, seers operate in the prophetic. "Formerly in Israel, when a man went to inquire of God, he spoke thus: 'Come, let us go to the seer'; for he who is now called a prophet was formerly called a seer." As a prophet and seer, I encounter God's prophetic voice mostly through visions and dreams, and sometimes, I encounter His voice in creation. I'm also strongly anointed with the gift of discerning of spirits, meaning, by the Holy Spirit, I can sense or feel the spiritual strongholds in certain geographical locations as well as in people, among other things.

I've written several books on the nature of prophets, seers, the gift of prophecy, and other gifts of the Holy Spirit and would humbly encourage you to read them for background information. As a seer entering Australia for the first time, right away I noticed the unique realm for visions and dreams that seemed to be draped over the land, or at least in all the places that I had visited.

I would loosely compare it to some scenes we read about in the book of Daniel in the Bible. For example, chapter 7 begins with, "In the first year of Belshazzar king of Babylon, Daniel had a dream and visions of his head while on his bed." What the prophet Daniel encountered here might have been "night visions," which some have described as the kind you have when you are half asleep and half awake. For that reason, it's harder to distinguish if they are dreams or visions.

Further in the chapter, Daniel used a series of phrases to explain his supernatural encounters such as, "I saw in my vision by night" (v. 2), "After this I looked" (v. 6), "After this I saw in the night visions" (v. 7), "I watched" (vv. 9, 11), "I was watching in the night visions" (v. 13), "the visions of my head troubled me" (v. 15), and "I was watching" (v. 21). All these referred to the visions and dreams he was having, and he described his God-given ability to freely watch and look at the many pictures and scenes of the future that were playing out around him. We read further in verse 16 how he "came near to one standing by" to get some kind of explanation. This happened to be an angel who then interpreted what he was dreaming about and supernaturally seeing. I might be stretching this, but it appeared as if a heavenly reality had superimposed itself over Daniel's earthly reality, and he was experiencing them both at the same time.

For Daniel, this seemed to be a very heavy experience, and I would not try to compare my situation to this. I used this narrative, however, because I recognized a similar pattern in parts of Australia where it felt like heaven and earth had simply merged together. As a result, my supernatural gifts from the Holy Spirit amplified noticeably. For example, I encountered the angelic in an intensified way and had uberrealistic dreams and visions from the Lord.

A few times, I was spiritually transported[5] into the nation by the Holy Spirit, and each time it happened right before I received an invitation to minister there. I'm still curious if my entire being was transported there or just my human spirit because it was so vividly real, although I lean toward it just being my human spirit. By the way, I don't actively teach on this topic for several reasons, even though there is a biblical precedent for it. (See 1 Kings 18:11–12; Ezekiel 3:12–14; 8:3; Acts 8:38–40; 2 Corinthians 12:2–4.)

I also experienced patterns of heavy warfare, a kind that was unique to this nation. I also saw certain false visions while in the land and thank God for His word because I wasn't swayed by them. At the same time, these false visions explained some areas of spiritual deception still holding on to pockets of First Nations culture and even some of Australia's more mystically inclined charismatics. All these things seemed unique to this nation, and I've had the privilege and challenge of experiencing it and then learning how to walk it out properly.

Surprisingly, many Australians didn't recognize or host a strong value for this spiritual blessing hovering over their nation. They seemed to approach this with more of a detached familiarity. For example, I've heard from several who've had authentic prophetic moments and points of discernment, only they didn't know what to do with these, so they just dismissed them. Others told me they saw things supernaturally and had genuine prophetic dreams but their church, family, friends, etc., made them feel weird and ungodly, and they took their denial as valid.

On the other extreme, some have mixed God's pure prophetic, including visions and dreams, with a kind of supernatural that the Bible does not condone. It has led to some weird theology, spiritual manipulation, supernatural extremism, false visions, false prophetic words, and a lack of conviction for sin. This always jades people toward anything truly prophetic and turns His church away from a biblically supernatural lifestyle. I believe strongly, however, that good teaching and solid community around this topic will bring it into order so that it blooms as God intended.

In early December 2019, I had a deep and powerful dream. I was standing in front of scores of people somewhere in Australia and shouting repeatedly at the top of my lungs, "He fights for you!" The quality of this dream was so compelling and urgent that the only thing I knew to do was to post the dream to my social media accounts. You could feel the weight of it, and many picked it up and shared it on their pages as people on social media often do. Within a week or two, Australia hit the news hard for a history-making megafire that ultimately burned fifty-three million acres, killed more than three billion animals, destroyed up to 3,500 buildings including homes, claimed the lives of thirty-four people, and cost the nation $78–$88 billion in property damage and loss.[6] This was the worst calculated damage of any fire in their history, yet God wanted them to know He was there in the middle of it and fighting for them. It was only the beginning of trouble, unfortunately. Right on the heels of the fire came the roar of the pandemic, causing even further trauma throughout the nation.

That prophetic word that came in the dream—He fights for you!—did not cease when that megafire or the pandemic ended. He is still fighting for Australia and fighting for His church there. And He is fighting hard for a reason. Although these have been largely underestimated, prophetic experiences, spiritual realities, and even slipping in and out of this overshadowing realm of visions and dreams seem to be an important part of their world. Perhaps this realm of visions and dreams was actually the "Dreamtime" these First Nations people encountered but failed to understand from God's view. Remember the story of Genesis and how the serpent came into the garden and deceived the first people? Did a similar event happen in the origins of Australia, thus setting a precedent for generations to come?

Either way, God is bringing this nation back to His original design. Firstly, He wants this nation's Indigenous to receive Jesus and His salvation plan and also to be restored to honor in the nation. First Nations people are important to the healing of any country because they were there first. This is just a basic principle. He also wants His church to become fluent in visions and dreams. In the

Bible, people and nations were saved as a result of this expression, which is the underpinning point of it all. He also instructed me to equip this nation specifically in my core teaching topics of prophets, visions and dreams, the seer anointing, discerning of spirits, etc., and thus complement other trusted teachers who are there and doing the same.

My battle there was not without purpose, and this story is still unfolding. Although this is an equipping book for all nations, I believe Australia is the catalyst that brought it forth. For this reason, I want to honor and thank the nation for hosting a supernatural climate that's been an absolute blessing and helped me to birth this weapon, *Awaken the Dreamscape*, and sow it into the earth.

AN OVERVIEW OF AWAKENING YOUR DREAMS

ONE

Awaken Your Dreams at Night

One week before the world spiraled into the crazy pandemic shutdown, the Holy Spirit put an unusual emphasis on dreams at night during an inner-healing-and-deliverance conference at Harvest Church in Turlock, California. When I opened the conference, He impressed upon my heart to pray for the conference attendees and awaken their dreams at night. I could tell there was something big about this prayer, only I didn't understand what. I was also unsure when to release this prayer, and so I waited for His perfect timing.

The conference was absolutely wild with miracles and hosted an unusual atmosphere of God's glory. Our first guest minister began the conference by taking us through an unusual teaching and deliverance prayer for our physical bones. It was on point, and I believe it paved the way for our second guest minister to step into one of her signature miracles. The Holy Spirit often had her pray for people with metal body parts, such as rods and pins, and He would miraculously turn these metal parts back to bone. I don't remember the exact points of healing and deliverance that I engaged by the power of the Spirit with the exception of one notable supernatural weight-loss miracle. But what I do remember is the Holy Spirit wouldn't let me rest until I prayed for everyone's dreams.

During the final session of the conference, I shared from the platform what He had instructed me to do. "The Holy Spirit wants me to pray for your dreams to awaken at night," I explained. As I began to pray for everyone, that same guest minister stood up and began waving at me wildly. She walked forward from her seat in the front row and verbalized her personal need for that miracle prayer because her dream life had virtually disappeared. She explained how it was a key area so that she would know what God was saying and doing, but her dream life had been turned off and she didn't know why. I stepped off the platform and walked toward her with my microphone in one hand and my other hand stretched toward her. I then rested my free hand gently on her shoulder and began to pray for her dreams to awaken at night. As I prayed, the power of God tangibly dropped upon us from heaven. We were both knocked backward, her back into the seats and me onto the ground. In addition, most of the attendees in the front row were also knocked down to the ground, but nobody was harmed by this power encounter.

Naturally, I felt the pressure to get up and go back to the platform to properly facilitate the session, only I couldn't physically wake myself up, even though I was awake on the inside. By then, my husband had come onto the platform just to stand in for us while all of this was happening. I finally did regain some awareness but could only crawl back to the front row and slump into my seat. The felt presence of God was so strong upon my person that, even after the session ended, I was still unable to function like normal. My team finally had to carry me out of the main sanctuary and deposit me onto a couch in the back room. I've never had an encounter this strong before and one that surprisingly targeted the awakening of our dreams at night.

I received numerous testimonies after the conference from people, including from that minister, who had stopped dreaming up until that targeted prayer but then started dreaming again. Others testified how they began dreaming much more vibrantly and frequently than before. "I'm fifty years old, and up until the time of the conference, I have only dreamed three times in my life that I could remember," explained one woman from Washington State. "Since that prayer, I've been regularly encountering God's voice and His healing and supernatural impartation inside my dreams at night."

The dream realm is a powerful theater for the voice of God. It is also fiercely contested by demons, which I'll explain more about throughout the chapters of this book. Regardless, I am persuaded that God wants to deposit powerful keys of freedom inside our dreams. Much like how I prayed for everyone at the conference, my prayer for you is for the power of the Holy Spirit to come upon you to awaken your dreams at night.

There Is a War for Your Dreams

When two or more countries go to war, they typically do so to take hold of that which belongs to another. The motive might be economic gain, territorial gain, or for reasons of religious or nationalistic superiority. It may also be for reasons of revenge or a defensive war to thwart an aggressor nation.[1] Whatever the reason, the end goal of war is to use violent force to achieve an objective.

Naturally speaking, there are wars between countries and civil and revolutionary wars inside countries. In addition, there are also spiritual wars, and we see many examples in the Bible. For example, when Elisha the prophet was being pursued by the Syrian army commander, the entire horizon filled up with angels in chariots to fight for him and the nation of Israel. (See 2 Kings 6:17.) The book of Daniel tells us about a war between Michael the Archangel and a demonic prince of Persia over matters concerning Daniel the prophet and the Israelites. (See Daniel 10:13.) A war also broke out in heaven between Michael and his angels and Satan and his angels, resulting in Satan and his demonic hosts being thrown out of heaven and down to the earth. (See Revelation 12:7.) We don't always consider our collective conflicts to be spiritually sourced, but this is often the case. Satan wars against us for personal gain. He has nothing of his own unless he can deceive people into giving it to him. He also wants revenge against God and, therefore, rages against humanity because human beings have been made in His image. Finally, he's terrified of our spiritual authority in Christ and engages in menacing defense wars to try to reduce and contain us. Consider that if something is not valuable, he wouldn't war for it. But if it's of value, he'll work overtime to try to take it. One of those areas of value is our dreams at night. Let me share a personal example.

I was watching the evening news, specifically a journalist by the name of Christiane Amanpour. As I watched her on television, I suddenly entered into a vision by the Holy Spirit. He began to speak to me about my next child, and I watched this journalist's name morph slightly and then turn into the name Christiana. By the way, I had incorrectly presumed she was British based on her accent but discovered soon after that her family was from the same country my husband was born in (Iran), although she had lived in both Tehran and England while growing up. I'm glad that I learned her true ethnicity as it abstractly helped confirm what I had seen from the Holy Spirit. Keep in mind that I'm unable to have children but had a similar experience with my first child, David. I had seen my son and heard his name in a vision a few years prior to conceiving him, which was an absolute miracle given my physical limitations.

Within a few years, I became pregnant with my daughter Christiana, but about mid-pregnancy, something began to happen to my thoughts and imagination. The part of my mind that generates pictures, referring to my imagination, seemed to have shut off, and I could no longer properly think or see with pictures. I would describe it as having a part of your mind go dark. In addition, I began experiencing a very debilitating insomnia. I stayed awake for days, an absolutely impossible number of days, and my tired mind and body began reacting with early contractions. I soon made my way to the doctor, feeling both mentally numb and extremely fatigued. She prescribed a pregnancy-safe sleep medication that helped me achieve just four-to-five hours of sleep a night, and I continued to feel as if parts of my mind were in the dark. Thankfully, I carried my daughter to term and gave birth to her via C-section. She was perfectly healthy, and my mind and ability to sleep went back to normal almost instantly. The situation was absolutely demonic, only I didn't realize the extent of it until it was over, and it wasn't over quite yet.

Within a few weeks of giving birth, I had an eerie, demonic dream. I dreamed that I was hopelessly addicted to prescription painkillers, then woke up from the dream confused and believing it was true. In reality, I was not abusing any pain medication and had not struggled with painkillers in the past. My doctor had prescribed me some pain medication that was common to take after a C-section, but I only took it when needed and never more than the recommended dose. Despite the facts, I was still convinced I was an addict and soon got rid of the prescription, thinking I might impulsively take too many. At this point, I recognized that something really bizarre was still happening to my mind as tormenting insomnia set in once again and now included panic attacks. I ended up taking a new medication, this time for what was believed to be a postpartum chemical imbalance. Despite the medication, I continued to struggle every day to get adequate sleep and to just maintain a semblance of normalcy.

Almost two years later, not much had changed. I was still on medication, not sleeping well, and trying to manage these abrupt panic attacks. The whole situation was absolutely tormenting. I was in a pastoral staff meeting at Harvest Church in Turlock and fled from a meeting in reaction to a panic attack. I was desperately tired and starting to give up hope. My best, most faith-filled prayers had not worked as far as I could tell, and I didn't know what to do. As I drove home in despair, I received an unexpected text from a woman that I knew.

> I had a vision from the Holy Spirit today. In the vision, I was pouring oil in your front yard and telling a mind-bending spirit to leave!

I was shocked at her words. Was God finally answering my prayer? I fully knew in my spirit that she was on target and texted her in return with this instruction,

> Please come over to my house and do exactly what you saw in the vision.

She did precisely that, and within a few hours of her performing this prophetic act[2] in my front yard, my mind returned to normal. I was healed and delivered by the power of Jesus Christ. I went back to my doctor, and within three weeks, I had weened myself off the medication, which is practically unheard of in that timeframe. My mind was finally illuminated again. My imagination began working like normal, I could see visions with clarity from the Holy Spirit, and my dream life came alive again, only more amplified. Even more shocking was the reality that none of this was physical but a wicked demon sent to mess with my mind and steal my sleep.

My sleep had been attacked for so long that I had almost forgotten what it was like to dream regularly. I didn't always know what my dreams meant, but I noticed a shift in the number of dreams I was having and in their overall prophetic nature. For example, I watched events happen in my dreams at night, and these dreams then unfolded while I was awake. So I began journaling some of these dreams in order to keep some kind of record. And since my deliverance was so dramatic, I began ministering out of my testimony of freedom and encountered volumes of suffering people who were also not sleeping and not dreaming for one reason or another. Was a demonic battle happening for our sleep? Was this battle for sleep really an attempt to steal our dreams at night?

By the power of the Holy Spirit, I began ministering in many astonishing deliverances to recover people's sleep and dreams. After this, I was fully convinced that Satan was petrified of our dream life. He is the thief of sleep and wants to destroy our ability to receive dreams from God. He knows his sinister plans could get exposed by God to an intercessor in a dream and then prayerfully crushed in response. I didn't fully understand the depths of what I was discovering about dreams, but the possibilities were thrilling. I also didn't understand the power of real, authentic dream interpretation until the Holy Spirit challenged me through a divine set-up.

Can You Interpret My Dream?

I was surprised to receive such an intriguing email from a well-known Christian who hosted a thriving ministry in Christian media. I had begun writing out my prophetic words for a popular online publication and was connected to this person through that ministry. This person clearly moved in the Holy Spirit's gift of prophecy. They most likely knew nearly every reputable prophet in America and maintained heaps of connections with prophets in other nations. For an unknown reason, this person reached out to me with their special request despite knowing so many others with much higher credentials. I now believe the Holy Spirit had quite purposely orchestrated this interaction. He was preparing me—more like provoking me—to step into a much deeper and more mysterious realm of the prophetic voice of God. He desires that this realm is revealed, taught, and activated in both you and me and in His church as a whole.

The email subject line went straight to the point. "Can you interpret my dream?" My curiosity was instantly piqued, and I eagerly opened it. The dream consisted of a few compactly written paragraphs yet was noticeably weighty with the Holy Spirit's anointing. The dream pointed toward something of national importance, only it was packaged by the Holy Spirit in a rich soup of symbols that seemed to cloak its true meaning.

During this time, my reputation as a seer prophet, speaker, and writer was just beginning to emerge past the sheltering borders of our first church campus in Turlock. (See 1 Samuel 9:9.) A prophet is one who is called by Jesus Christ alongside the other governing offices of the apostle, evangelist, pastor, and teacher. Ephesians 4:11 says, "And He Himself gave some to be apostles, some prophets, some evangelists, and some pastors and teachers." A person is branded as a seer prophet by how they primarily receive prophetic words from God, which is mostly through visions and dreams. In other words, they see the word of the Lord much more than they hear the word of the Lord, and they are typically skilled at interpreting dreams. As I was now learning to swim the untamed and dangerous waters of public ministry as a recognized and emerging seer prophet, this request seemed to validate my calling and point to greater ministry ahead.

With zeal, I quickly reviewed the contents of the dream and just paid attention to my overall first impression. I didn't take much time to pray or ask the dreamer questions to narrow down the context nor did I utilize any proven process for biblical-dream interpretation.

With haste and excitement, I responded to the dreamer with my best opinion of what the dream could mean. I want to emphasize that I gave this individual my opinion about the meaning of the dream, and I did not provide a Holy Spirit–led interpretation. This person, who was both prophetic and discerning, saw right through my attempt instantly. They promptly emailed back and wrote, "Thanks for trying, but that's not it."

I was embarrassed by their response, but the situation served a much higher purpose. It effectively pushed me to seek out and learn biblical dream interpretation. Frankly put, we don't just give our own hasty opinions about the meaning of dreams. A specific process undergirds true Holy Spirit–inspired dream interpretation, a process that has to be studied, developed, and practiced over time.

With that, I began earnestly seeking out reputable and biblical instruction about dream interpretation. I then devoted an entire year of study to this topic alone and have continued to study and practice dream interpretation ever since. I've since recognized that too many people hold little value or understanding about dreams in general. They haven't been taught to see their dreams as important and have ignored an entire channel for the voice of God in their life.

Many of our dreams at night are a gift from God, but a gift needs to be unwrapped and examined to see the treasure inside. This book will awaken you to an abundance of supernatural encounters with God inside your dreams. It will also start you on the road to correct dream interpretation. To begin, let's first discuss who can have visions and dreams from the Holy Spirit and why.

Who Can Have Visions and Dreams?

When the Holy Spirit was poured out upon the believers in Acts 2, not only did they receive power, but they were awakened to the prophetic realm of visions and dreams. The prophet Joel in the Old Testament prophesied into an amazing shift that would change the entire prophetic order as they knew it. He predicted God's prophetic voice would no longer be restrained to just the prophets but would emerge in the life of every believer because of the outpouring.of the Holy Spirit.

> And it shall come to pass afterward
> That I will pour out My Spirit on all flesh;
> Your sons and your daughters shall prophesy,
> Your old men shall dream dreams,
> Your young men shall see visions.
>
> Joel 2:28

Joel's prophecy came to life when the disciples waited in the upper room in Jerusalem for "the promise of the Father" after the death and resurrection of Jesus Christ. (See Acts 1:4.) As they worshipped and waited, suddenly a sound came from heaven, and then, a powerful wind filled the room. Tongues of fire appeared and then rested upon each individual so that they all spoke in other tongues. Their collective sound arrested the attention of the visiting Jews to Jerusalem that day because they supernaturally heard the praises of God pouring from the lips of the disciples in each of their native tongues. As thousands of Jews gathered to investigate the phenomenon, the apostle Peter rose to explain this to the crowd. He proclaimed to everyone how this is that which was spoken by the prophet Joel. And beginning with Joel 2:28, he preached the gospel of Jesus Christ to the crowd, with more than three thousand souls turning to faith in Christ. In addition to mass salvation, an outstanding new prophetic order emerged. The prophetic voice of God was no longer limited to just the prophets. If you were a believer in Jesus, you, too, could have visions and dreams and prophesy by the unction of the Holy Spirit.

Visions and dreams are both the picture language of God, but they do have distinct differences. To understand the nature and composition of dreams, we will first need to comprehend the nature of visions.

Visions and Dreams Are a Separate Language

One of the most common ways God communicated His will to people in the Bible was through visions and dreams. Visions were portrayed as vivid apparitions that appeared primarily during waking hours, while dreams occurred while sleeping. Visions in the Bible came in a variety of forms, such as waking visions, trances, and even night visions. A night vision, also called a vision of the night, is when a person experiences a vision while dreaming. "Then the secret was revealed to Daniel in a night vision. So Daniel blessed the God of heaven" (Daniel 2:19); "In a dream, in a vision of the night, when deep sleep falls upon men, while slumbering on their beds" (Job 33:15). To further explain night visions, some have described them as the kind you might have when you are half asleep and half awake.[3] Visions in the Bible involved natural or supernatural settings, and the individual experiencing the vision was either a participant or an observer. In the Old Testament, visions were so important that their absence signaled relational trouble between the Israelite community and God. (See 1 Samuel 3:1 and Proverbs 29:18.)

Those who experienced visions as a means of God revealing information to them included Abraham, Jacob, the false prophet Balaam, the prophet Samuel, the prophet Micaiah, and Eliphaz the Temanite. (See Genesis 15; 46:1–4; Numbers 24; 1 Samuel 3; 1 Kings 22:17–28; and Job 4:13–21.) In 2 Samuel 7:1–17, Nathan the prophet was told in a vision that King David's throne would be established forever and one of his descendants would construct a permanent temple for God in Jerusalem.

In Ezekiel 1, Ezekiel had several truths and future events revealed to him through visions. He was shown the glory and throne of God, was informed of wicked acts of idolatry inside Jerusalem's temple, and also saw a valley of dry bones come together to form a living army that represented the regathering of Israel. (See Ezekiel 8 and 37.) Daniel experienced several visions, including one that revealed four impending world empires, the Ancient of Days seated on His throne, and events to come in the last days. (See Daniel 7:1–10 and Daniel 10.) Isaiah was told in visions about the future kingdoms of Judah, Babylon, and Jerusalem. (See Isaiah 1, 21, and 22.) Many of the Old Testament's minor prophets, including Amos, Obadiah, Nahum, Habakkuk, and Zechariah, received visions concerning the future.

The contents of visions shift noticeably between the Old Testament and the New Testament. That shift was seen mostly in the focus and purpose of the conversation. Instead of laments and judgments over the idolatry of Israel, God communicated through visions about the salvation and care of people and in matters about His church on the earth. For example, Ananias was told in a vision exactly where to find Saul and then instructed to supernaturally heal Saul's eyes, which had been blinded during an encounter with Jesus. (See Acts 9:10–19.) Cornelius was a Gentile, which means anyone who was not a Jew. Even so, Cornelius feared and worshipped God and was directed in a vision to find the apostle Peter at an exact location and to hear his words. Just before Cornelius and his delegation arrived, Peter received a dramatic vision showing him not to reject people who were not Jews from hearing the gospel. As a result, in Acts 10, Cornelius and his household became the first Gentile converts to Christianity. We also notice that in the book of Revelation, the apostle John received instructions through visions concerning each of the seven churches of Asia Minor. He also had amazing visions that detailed the end times and return of Jesus Christ.

Both Joel 2:28 and Acts 2:17 state that *young* men will have visions and *old* men will have dreams. This really points to the maturity needed to comprehend dream language. The nature of visions and dreams can be understood best if you think of each as a spiritual, actually a picture, language. Visions, then, are typically the more simple and comprehensible language while dreams are typically the richer and more complex language of the two.

When it came to visions, even in their different forms and their interpretation, I was fluent. I nearly always understood visions even if those came to me in a more complex way. In addition, the Holy Spirit had taken time with me at the onset of my ministry to train my spiritual eyes to see what He was saying through visions, usually for the purpose of intercession and personal ministry. I wrote more about this in my book *Prophetic Secrets*. He would specifically highlight a person to me and ask, "What do you see?" He was prompting me to identify these short, simple visions that He was giving to me that related to that person prophetically. These brief visions would come to me as a quick picture right in front of me, or they would appear instantly in my imagination. I would then either intercede for that person or approach them for ministry, based on the information that I supernaturally saw. He was teaching me how to identify His communication through visions and then how to effectively process their contents. He was making the following Scriptures come alive: "Moreover the word of the LORD came to me, saying, 'Jeremiah, what do you see?' And I said, 'I see a branch of an almond tree'" (Jeremiah 1:11). "And the LORD said to me, 'Amos, what do you see?' And I said, 'A plumb line. . . .'" (Amos 7:8). "And he said to me, 'What do you see?' So I answered, 'I see a flying scroll. Its length is twenty cubits and its width ten cubits'" (Zechariah 5:2).

Since I didn't understand the differences between visions and dreams, I neglected to pursue a deeper understanding of dreams in general. I presumed that dreams were as easy as visions to understand, and if I didn't understand a dream, I would invalidate it for one reason or another. I never considered that visions and dreams were separate languages and that dreams could be more complex, for that matter. I also didn't know about the process for dream interpretation until I was challenged to study the topic more in depth. As I studied, I recognized that the impact of dreams and their meanings could be lost and that we have a great need for dream interpreters.

• KINGDOM PRINCIPLES •

1. The dream realm is a powerful theater for the voice of God. He will deposit powerful keys of freedom inside our dreams.
2. Satan is petrified of our dream life. He is a thief of sleep and wants to destroy our ability to receive dreams from God.
3. Many of our dreams at night are a gift from God, but a gift needs to be unwrapped and examined in order to see the treasure inside.

4. Distinguishing in both Joel 2:28 and Acts 2:17 that *young* men will have visions and *old* men will have dreams was really pointing to the maturity needed to comprehend dream language.

5. Visions and dreams are both the picture language of God, but they do have distinct differences.

● THOUGHTS FOR REFLECTION ●

1. Are you in a battle to sleep at night? After reading this chapter, would you say it's a natural or demonic battle?

2. Have you ever had a vision from the Holy Spirit? What was the outcome?

3. Do you ever have prophetic dreams about the future? If so, do you record your dreams in a journal?

4. Visions and dreams are both the picture language of God, but there are differences. How have you noticed these differences?

5. Have you ever tried to interpret someone's dream? If so, was your interpretation accurate? How would you know?

TWO

Dreams Need an Interpreter

Growing up as a child, I had a dream with a recurring theme. It highly disturbed me, only I didn't know what it meant. It involved black widow spiders, and then elements of the dreams would come in themes of two. For example, I would dream about two black widow spiders but in different contexts, or I would dream about two trees, and the two trees were full of black widow spiders. I know now that these dreams actually came from God, and He was sounding off about a critical area of my life that needed His divine intervention. His message to me was hidden from my understanding, largely due to the symbolism and because I didn't know Him, let alone know anyone who could interpret my dreams.

While studying Christian dream symbols and biblical dream interpretation, I learned one meaning for black widows. In dreams, they might point to some kind of witchcraft or the occult. The Bible, which is our foundation for dream interpretation, connects deception with the spider's web and how a web might be formed by people to capture you for nefarious purposes. Isaiah 59: 5 says, "They hatch vipers' eggs and weave the spider's web; he who eats of their eggs dies, and from that which is crushed a viper breaks out."

The meaning is also banked upon the stereotypical behavior of female widows who spin their webs to catch their unsuspecting prey.

They might cannibalize their mates, then devour some of their hatchlings.[1] In other words, the darker shades of the occult seek to capture people in a web of spiritual deception, destroy marital covenant and covenant with God, and maliciously pursue children for destruction.

For context, I had grown up in the Mormon church but gave my life to the true Jesus as a freshman in college. Mormons often profess to be Christians by saying they believe in Jesus, only the Jesus they believe in is not the same Jesus we see in the Bible.[2] This made my decision a big deal because it was in total opposition to everything I had been raised to believe. Adding to my scandalous decision, I also received the baptism of the Holy Spirit and began speaking with other tongues within moments of my conversion. There was no going back to the Mormon church after that. Roughly fifteen years later, my personal testimony expanded after my family's generational roots in Freemasonry were exposed through the divine intervention of the Holy Spirit. I experienced a powerful deliverance once a hidden family curse that stemmed from Freemasonry was broken off my life. The results were amazing. Once the curse was broken, my ministry expanded in every way.

I had concluded the two black widow spiders in my childhood dreams represented these two occult orders, but why would I dream about two trees full of them? The answer to my question came after a life-changing and unusual heart-healing encounter initiated by the Holy Spirit. The impact of this caused my testimony to greatly expand once again. I have written in much more detail what undergirded my trauma-induced amnesia and extreme dissociation in my book *The Inner Healing and Deliverance Handbook*.

Large gaps of time from my growing-up years seemed to be missing. I couldn't remember what happened during these time periods and thought this was normal and never questioned it. The short story is that when I turned forty-seven years old and in response to this deeply transforming Holy Spirit encounter, my buried memories finally surfaced. Those memories involved some family members subjecting me to violent satanism, sorcery, and ritual rape, and then being trafficked within an occult pedophile network by my biological father. It's a typical psychological pattern for all those who've survived this kind of horror, only it's a story not typically understood or even believed by those who've never experienced it. Although my story is extreme, my healing journey has been absolutely miraculous. With that said, I finally understood the dreams about the two trees full of black widow spiders. Those trees in my dreams were pointing to family trees that had been infested on various levels with the darkest aspects of the occult.

To this day, I absolutely hate black widow spiders and reactively smash them to smithereens whenever I find them on or around my property. My childhood dreams about these venomous creatures told the entire story, only there was no dream interpreter nor any thought to seek one out. I've wondered since if I would have received earlier intervention if there had been one, but only God knows the answer to that question. He was sounding off loud and clear about my horrific situation, only I didn't comprehend the message because of a significant language barrier.

After much research and based on my personal experience, I've concluded that He actively speaks to most of mankind in dreams, even those who don't know Him yet. And when necessary, He sends dreams to people with the intent of leading them into salvation and deliverance. "I dreamed multiple times I had died and was escorted by an angel to the gate of heaven," one man explained. "After a verification process, I was denied entrance and knew I was being sent to hell." Each time he dreamed this dream, he woke up in a cold sweat with heart-pounding terror. His dream of going to hell finally stopped when he surrendered his life to Christ. This person's story concluded well, but for others, such dreams can be lost in translation unless a solid Christian interpreter can intervene.

Nations Are Saved through Dreams

In the Bible, Joseph was clearly Jacob's most-loved son. He was the son of Jacob's old age, and Jacob gave him a gorgeous coat of many colors, something he didn't do for his eleven other sons. We read all about it in Genesis 37 and how Joseph proudly wore his colorful coat while giving his father bad reports about his older brothers. His siblings were understandably enraged, and then he shared a few dreams that caused their jealousy to intensify. He dreamed that he and his brothers were bundling wheat together and that his bundle stood upright while his brothers' bundles reverently bowed down low to his bundle. He dreamed a second time. This time, he dreamed that the sun and the moon, which represented his father and mother, and also eleven stars bowed down to honor him. When Joseph shared his dreams that clearly implied that he would someday reign over his family, his father sternly rebuked him, and his brothers began plotting his murder.

To the ancient Israelite, dreams and dream language were taken seriously and still are by observant Jews and much of the modern Middle-Eastern world.[3] Joseph's dreams were unnerving to his family, largely because of the high value they put on the dream realm. They believed their dreams were spiritually sourced and therefore something to pay attention to. For that reason, because of his dreams, Joseph was removed from the stability of his family and sold into slavery in Egypt at the hands of his irate brothers. While in slavery, he was falsely accused of attempted rape by his master's wife after he refused her sexual advances. As a result, he was unjustly confined to Pharaoh's prison, but his ability to interpret dreams earned him an early release and a huge promotion.

Pharoah's cupbearer and baker had offended the king, and both were jailed in the same place as Joseph. Historically, a cupbearer was a highly ranked official and was responsible for serving the wine at the king's table. Since rulers were concerned about being poisoned, the cupbearer would taste test the wine to make sure it was safe to drink. Good and trustworthy cupbearers were then loyal and dependable individuals positioned to influence the king.[4] While in prison, both the cupbearer and baker had troubling dreams on the same night. Joseph noticed how troubled they were and asked them for an explanation. They said, "We each have had a dream, and there is no interpreter of it" (Genesis 40:8).

Take notice of their complaint. They had dreams but couldn't resolve them *because there was no interpreter*. Joseph listened to the details and instructed them that interpretations belong to God and then proceeded to interpret their dreams. The baker's dream revealed that he would be executed within three days, which is exactly what happened. The cupbearer's dream revealed that he would be restored to his position within three days, and this happened as well. Upon the cupbearer's exit from prison, Joseph asked him to remember him and appeal to Pharaoh on his behalf, only he forgot to do so.

Two years later, Pharaoh had a set of dreams that greatly troubled his spirit, only he didn't know their meanings. He first dreamed of seven fat cows that came up from a river and then fed blissfully in a meadow. Then seven other cows came up after them, only they were emaciated and gaunt, and they swallowed up the seven fat cows. He had a second dream about seven heads of grain on a stalk that were plump and healthy, followed by seven scrawny heads of grain that sprang up and swallowed the seven plump heads of grain. He recited his dreams to all of Egypt's magicians and wise men, "but there was no one who could interpret them for Pharaoh" (Genesis 41:8). Take notice again that among all of Pharaoh's sorcerers and advisors, there was no interpreter.

At the cupbearer's advice, Pharaoh sent for Joseph to see if he could interpret the dreams. Joseph first acknowledged that God was the Source of Pharaoh's dreams and also their interpretation. Based on the pattern of symbols in the dreams, Joseph foretold that seven years of abundance would come to Egypt, followed by seven years of severe famine. Joseph counseled Pharaoh to put a wise man in charge of Egypt to prepare the land to be sufficiently sustained during the coming famine. Recognizing the Spirit of God speaking through Joseph, Pharaoh promoted him to prime minister of Egypt and put him in charge of the tremendous task.

Joseph's original dreams about ruling over his family ended up coming true. He became second in command over Egypt and saved the nation and its economy. His position also reunited him with his family when they came to Egypt seeking food supplies. Not only did he provide for them and thus save them from starvation, but his actions ultimately saved the entire lineage of Israel. These events took place because God was speaking to mankind in dreams, and in this situation, there was an interpreter. Is He saving nations and people today through dreams? The answer is yes! He continues to speak in our dreams in the night, and cultures that host a value for dreams are laying hold of eternal salvation as a result.

Have You Seen the Man in White?

A now-familiar testimony for Muslims and other people across the Middle East and in countries closed to Christianity is to share how they converted to Jesus because of a dream.[5] The dream I'm referring to has commonly centered around a "man in white" who they believe is Jesus, and something about the dream compels them to become a Christian even in the most dangerous of circumstances. Here are a few examples.

An Islamic militant fighter who massacred Christians ultimately converted to the faith of his victims after having this kind of dream. Gina Fadely, a former director with Youth With A Mission (YWAM), shared the following testimony on The Voice of the Martyrs Radio Network. She described how one of YWAM's workers was put in contact with an ISIS fighter who had brutally murdered a number of Christians. He confessed that he found a deep satisfaction in killing them until he encountered Jesus in a dream.

> "He told this YWAM leader that he had begun having dreams of this man in white who came to him and said, 'You are killing my people.' He started to feel really sick and uneasy about what he was doing," Fadely continued. "The fighter said just before he killed one Christian, the man said, 'I know you will kill me, but I give to you my Bible.' The Christian was killed and this ISIS fighter actually took the Bible and began to read it. In another dream, Jesus asked him to follow him and he was now asking to become a follower of Christ and to be discipled."[6]

As another committed Shiite, Jaffar joined the fight against the Sunni-initiated Islamic State (ISIS). He became disheartened after watching Shiite army leaders steal the wages of their men and when his best friend died from a gunshot wound. Jaffar suffered a serious leg injury only forty-five days into his contract and was forced to return home. Emotionally and spiritually broken, he began to cry out to God in desperation, asking Him to make Himself known. That night, he received his answer in a stunning dream.

> He was perched on a narrow bridge wide enough for only one. Beneath him was an abyss of smoke and fire, radiating heat upward. He could hear the screams of others behind him as the bridge crumbled beneath their feet and they plunged into the gulf below. Terrified, he took one careful step after another.
>
> After reaching a door at the end of the bridge, he knocked and a man in a white garment opened the door. "Who are you?" Jaffar asked. The man told him he was the owner of the door and invited him in. He warned Jaffar, however, that if he stepped through the door, he could never go back out. Knowing what was behind him, he stepped over the threshold. [7]

In the dream, Jaffar was filled with unexplainable peace, and then he woke up. In response, he proceeded to engage in a personal journey to find Jesus, and through a former employer who happened to be a Christian, he wholeheartedly accepted Jesus despite very real threats of persecution and death. There are thousands upon thousands of testimonies about people converting to Christ in these circumstances because of a dream. One family of ministers that I know who's reached into these nations for decades has confirmed the accuracy of these reports. "Muslims will commonly dream about a man in white, and He instructs them what to do next," one of the ministers said. "They come asking, 'Have you seen the man in white?' and we know exactly what to do."

From ancient times, Middle Easterners have esteemed dreams to be of high value. "A well-known hadith[8] teaches, 'The dreams of the faithful are prophetic,'" wrote Nabeel Qureshi in his book *Seeking Allah, Finding Jesus*. "In fact, dreams are the only means I know of by which the average Muslim expects to hear directly from God."[9] This same man found Jesus and converted to Christianity after years of debate with a Christian friend and in response to a series of dreams, one of which used symbols and meanings common to their Muslim faith and culture yet clearly was a message from Jesus Christ. He later became a Christian apologist before dying of cancer in 2017.

A culture that values dreams is a culture that Jesus can speak to. But like those in false and even violent religions, they cannot fathom that Jesus wants to be their Savior and Lord. Through dreams, however, God is reaching these kinds of people and turning them around. Sadly, some cultures dismiss the notion that God wants to reach us in our dreams. Western philosophy and even westernized Christianity, for example, have filtered out most of the spiritual aspects of dreams and ultimately robbed us of His voice in this manner.

Don't Be Robbed by Culture

How can a dream be so powerful as to convert another human being from one way of believing to having faith in Jesus Christ? Are dreams really that powerful? Consider what Job had to say about dreams:

> For God may speak in one way, or in another,
> Yet man does not perceive it.
> In a dream, in a vision of the night,
> When deep sleep falls upon men,
> While slumbering on their beds,
> Then He opens the ears of men,
> And seals their instruction.
> In order to turn man from his deed,
> And conceal pride from man,
> He keeps back his soul from the Pit,
> And his life from perishing by the sword.
>
> Job 33:14–18

When we are asleep, God speaks to us in dreams because He has a captive audience incapable of shutting down His voice. We can't dismiss Him or tune Him out during the night in the same way that we often do during the day. In a dream, He can also communicate directly to our spirits and thus bypass our logic or rational thinking that stands in the way of our spiritual understanding. At night, our body might be sleeping, but our spirit remains awake. And God, who is Spirit, will communicate to us Spirit to spirit and reach our very core.

The contents of most dreams can be compared in structure to the parables in the Bible. A parable is an earthly and symbolic story or illustration that has a heavenly meaning. For example, He spoke various parables in the Bible about the kingdom of God. One described it as a mustard seed, the least of all the seeds, which a man sowed into a field that grew to be the greatest of all the trees (Matthew 13:31–32). He spoke another parable on the same topic: "The Kingdom of Heaven is like the yeast a woman used in making bread. Even though she put only a little yeast in three measures of flour, it permeated every part of the dough" (Matthew 13:33 NLT).

Jesus spoke many such parables and explained to His disciples that His use of parables "had a two-fold purpose: to reveal the truth to those who wanted to know it and to conceal the truth from those who were indifferent."[10] (See also Matthew 13:10–17.) Dreams are night parables that use symbols and metaphorical stories that conceal a message from those who are either ignorant or indifferent but are unveiled to those committed to searching them out. We read in Proverbs 25:2, "It is the glory of God to conceal a matter, but the glory of kings is to search out a matter." This tells us that it's possible to get to the divinely concealed meaning of most of our dreams if we are diligent enough to search it out.

All too often, we've dismissed our dreams because they seem nonsensical. Sometimes we chalk it up to eating something unhealthy too late in the evening or something we watched on television. For example, if you had a random dream that you were flying into outer space, this dream definitely doesn't make any sense. It's memorable and might captivate your imagination for a few hours or more, but unless you search it out or get help from a seasoned interpreter, you might lose the gift offered to you inside this dream. This dream, by the way, is one of many common dreams to show you that you are being positioned to head into higher spiritual experiences, a higher promotion, and/or higher creativity in an area of your life.

Dismissing your dreams is like leaving a really valuable gift from God unopened and ignored. This response also stems from how our western culture has superimposed itself on the way we think about dreams in general. Westernized thinking has largely been influenced by Greek thinking and hinges on facts, logic, and reason. Eastern thinking is typically more abstract, experiential, and spiritual but not necessarily Christian. Some would argue that western culture, especially in America, is a spiritual culture because of this nation's Christian foundation. However, Christianity is reduced to a religion without power when there is not an active supernatural expression of the Holy Spirit.

An American Christian writer who was probably a cessationist in his theology shared an article online. A cessationist believes that the Holy Spirit's supernatural expression through individuals ceased with the end of the apostolic age and the completion of New Testament revelation.[11] He, too, was examining the "man in white" dreams of those Muslims who came to Christ in response. Surprisingly, he questioned the validity of their collective dream experiences, even inferring their dreams might not have come from God but were possibly suggested or the by-product of impressionable minds, although he didn't question their decisions for Christ. This is a clear example of what I mean when westernized thinking has superimposed itself over the Bible and what God has historically done and continues to do with dreams. Consider that the Bible is an eastern Hebraic book and that our Greek thinking and subsequent cultural philosophy came later. This way of thinking is valuable but not when it comes to properly sourcing our dreams and actually interpreting them.

The Bible Is Our Foundation for Interpretation

"I had a really crazy dream, and I think I have the interpretation," she told me excitedly. "Can I get your feedback?" Several years later, I now realize that she probably didn't want my honest feedback. What she wanted was my validation of her process and here's why. She shared the dream with me and the interpretation, along with her process of discovering it. While she was sharing, I almost gasped when she explained how she arrived at the meaning of the main symbol in her dream. She showed me an occult book and remarked, "This is the only book that addresses this symbol in a way that seems to fit."

I was patient and kind in my response, but you can probably guess what I said. I can't say this enough to Christians who are interested in knowing what their dreams mean. We need to make the Bible our foundation and guide for interpretation and not rely on ungodly sources, unverified sources, occult or secular dream dictionaries, etc., even when we're stumped on the meaning of a dream. Over time, this same woman never fully separated herself from elements of witchcraft, although she was a professing Christian. Despite her wealth and status, she often appeared to be in spiritual confusion and spent her time chasing fantasy spiritual assignments that she believed were from the Holy Spirit. Let's make sure that we have this principle in proper order so we don't get confused and waste years, even decades, of our life in spiritual delusion.

Most of these kinds of problems stem from a lack of teaching. People want to know what their dreams mean, but they have no idea how to properly seek that out. In ignorance, they might attempt to source the meanings of dream symbols through random internet sites.

Just for fun, I googled, "What does it mean when you see a bear in your dream?" The first source by a so-called expert said this kind of dream has to do with hunting. The expert explained, "Bears are hunters, so what are you hunting?" Another secular dream expert described how bears are wild animals and dreaming about one is pointing to something wild and untamed in you. And then another provided several ideas about bears appearing in dreams, only most of them were the spiritualized opinion of the writer.

On the surface, these possible meanings seem interesting, but there was a soulish quality to all of it. The Bible, Jesus, or His Holy Spirit was not mentioned in the discussions, which should be the first red flag. As addressed earlier in this chapter, Joseph taught us biblical guidelines for interpreting dreams, specifically that true interpretations come from God. This is clear instruction to avoid unsanctified dream specialists.

Based on this guideline, I decided not to pursue writing a dream dictionary. Many are already available from credible Christian leaders, and in my opinion, creating one more dictionary would be reinventing the wheel. Secondly, such dictionaries are not primary but secondary sources for interpretation. They are interesting and, at times, helpful, but the Bible is our foundation and guide for dream interpretation, and I believe these authors would concur.

The late John Paul Jackson also warned us about relying on popular dream interpretation models as proposed by secular psychiatrists Sigmund Freud, Carl Jung, and Fritz Perls. (By the way, John Paul Jackson was one of the best dream interpretation instructors that I've ever studied.) These psychiatrists believed that your dreams revealed aspects of your soul and viewed them as a means to psychoanalyze you. He stated that the problem with using their models for dream interpretation is that you never get the same interpretation when you pair them with dreams in the Bible, dreams that were interpreted for us.

"Freud taught that dreams tend to reveal our latent sexual desires, whereas Jung taught that most of the elements within a dream are there to reveal more about our inner-self," wrote Doug Addison in his book *Understand Your Dreams Now*. "They taught that the dream resides inside of you and is working its way out" as a means to reveal and heal your psyche.[12] Biblical and Hebraic thinking is the opposite. The dream isn't coming from inside you but from the outside of you, actually from God, to reveal things about you and things to come in the future.

To illustrate, Jackson shared a woman's dream he heard on the radio and the secular dream interpreter's response:

A woman dreamt she was looking out of her kitchen window to the backyard where the swing set of her children were and saw spiders all over the ground. She went to the store to get something to kill the spiders and the store manager said, "You don't need something to kill the spiders. You need something to kill what the spiders are eating and living off of."

The secular dream interpreter said, 'This is you. This is your inner child. The swing set represents your inner child. The spiders represent the myriad of things in your life that are trying to keep your inner child from rising up and you living a life so your inner child can develop and can become free. The things the store manager wanted you to get were to get you to recognize what is keeping your inner child from rising up.'"[13]

Jackson used this illustration to support his point. The radio interpreter had echoed a popular sentiment by secular psychiatrists who believed dreams were most likely about your inner child issues. Only this dream was not about her inner child at all. The dream was about problems affecting her actual children, and the spiders represented occult issues. These spiders were little, tiny occult issues coming at them from everywhere. The store manager represented Jesus, and His instruction was to kill whatever the demons were living off so the demons wouldn't affect her children anymore. Jackson finished by saying that the woman was stumped at his remarks and that she thought the dream was really about her children and why they were having such severe night terrors.

Hopefully, you were able to understand how Jackson arrived at the interpretation of the woman's dream and the drastic differences between his interpretation and the radio host's. Your foundation for dream interpretation matters and will skew the outcome accordingly. A misinterpreted dream leaves the person with a sense of unfulfillment or dissatisfaction. It's like going to the ATM to withdraw money, but no money comes out. It's like the response of the Christian media person when I gave my opinion of their dream after they received a wrong interpretation. Their response was, "That's not it!"

When you receive the correct interpretation, your spirit awakens and syncs to it. Perhaps you've never interpreted your dreams or the dreams of others before in this manner. In the next section, you'll learn the building blocks for biblical dream interpretation so that you can get started.

• KINGDOM PRINCIPLES •

1. God actively speaks to most of mankind in dreams, even those who don't know Him yet. Without a dream interpreter, however, such dreams could be lost in translation.

2. Cultures that have a deep value for dreams are laying hold of eternal salvation as a result. Many people have testified how they turned from false and even violent religions to Jesus Christ, all because of a dream.

3. Westernized philosophy and even westernized Christianity have filtered out most of the spiritual aspects of dreams and robbed us of His voice in this manner. Instead of being motivated to search out a dream, we've culturally dismissed our dreams as nonsensical and perhaps the result of something unhealthy that we ate.

4. Dreams are night parables that use symbols and metaphorical stories that conceal a message. The message will be lost to those who are ignorant or indifferent but unveiled to those committed to searching it out.

5. When it comes to dream interpretation, the Bible is our foundation and guide. We should not rely on ungodly sources, unverified sources, occult or secular dream dictionaries, etc., even when we're stumped on the meaning of a dream as these sources will negatively alter the meaning.

• THOUGHTS FOR REFLECTION •

1. Why would God send dreams to people who don't know Him yet, and then send dreams they might not understand?

2. Is God still saving people and nations through dreams? Why or why not?

3. Why are there not more Christian dream interpreters?

4. Some cultures value dreams and others don't. Which culture has most influenced you?

5. When it comes to dream interpretation, why does the foundation for interpretation matter? What happens to the interpretation when we don't operate from a biblical foundation?

THE BUILDING BLOCKS FOR DREAM INTERPRETATION

THREE

God Deposits His Plans in Our Dreams

In 2008, America went through a serious economic recession and housing crash, largely due to widespread predatory lending practices in which various lenders gave loans to homebuyers who could not afford them. The fallout created a ripple effect throughout the entire global financial system, even causing the stock market to crash. Banks in the United States and around the world began to fail, triggering one of the worst financial downturns since 1929.[1] Reactionary fear swept the nation, and people began hoarding money. Many Christians withheld tithes and offerings from their churches, and some churches failed from the dwindling income and financial pressure. During this season, my husband and I learned to have faith in God on an entirely new level. God was perfectly faithful to speak His instructions to us, and He spoke one night to my husband through a pivotal dream.

In the dream, Ron had inherited a church located across the street from our original church campus in downtown Turlock. He had also inherited an associate pastor. Ron went over to see his newly acquired church to find out who his new associate was. To his surprise, it was the late Reverend Kenneth E. Hagin. Ron thought, *Oh no! What am I going to do with him? He's so old!* Ron was busy trying to figure out what task he could assign him to during the Sunday church service and decided that he should receive the offering. When Ron asked him, Ken Hagin responded with the familiar, "Yep, yep, yep," and that was the end of the dream.

To provide some background, Kenneth E. Hagin was an influential preacher born on August 20, 1917, in McKinney, Texas. He was extremely ill as a child, having a deformed heart and what was believed to be an incurable blood disease. At age fifteen, he became bedridden and appeared to be dying. In April 1933, during a remarkable conversion experience, he described dying three times in ten minutes and, each time, experiencing the fires of hell but then coming back to life. He was miraculously healed in August 1934 by revelation of having faith in God's Word. [2]

Two years after his miracle healing, he preached his first sermon as the pastor of a small community church in Roland, Texas. He then went on to be the father of the Word of Faith movement, a movement with worldwide adherents who ascribed to his teachings about faith in God's Word. He often quoted Mark 11:23, "For verily I say unto you, That whosoever shall say unto this mountain, Be thou removed, and be thou cast into the sea; and shall not doubt in his heart, but shall believe that those things which he saith shall come to pass; he shall have whatsoever he saith" (KJV).

As new Christians, my husband and I cut our spiritual baby teeth on Ken Hagin's teachings, specifically how to overcome problems by speaking out faith-filled words based upon the promises of God. If we were sick, for instance, we would pray by saying out loud the Bible verses that addressed healing, but we would say them as if we were already healed. For example, we would simply say, "Thank you, Jesus, that by Your stripes, we are healed" (1 Peter 2:24). Ron and I also attended his church briefly while we were students at Oral Roberts University in Tulsa. Like most movements, there were some growing excesses among the Word of Faith adherents. Regardless, the teaching of faith enabled us to overcome many impossible obstacles both personally and in ministry.

At the time of Ron's dream, the mountain that needed to move was the financial fallout of the recession that had alarmingly reduced the tithes and offerings at our church. As I stated earlier, the Word of Faith movement had excesses. An undercurrent of pride and a misuse of faith teachings to gain wealth and status for selfish reasons permeated the movement. Because of these extremes, my husband considered moving away from some of the core principles, only this dream caused him to reconsider them once again.

Ron explained, "When I woke up from the dream and prayed into its meaning, I felt the Lord speak His counsel to my heart." He instructed me by saying, "Faith never gets old, and faith always receives the offering." In other words, you don't move on from having faith in God's promises to something else. With that instruction, Ron was renewed in hope and motivated to teach, encourage, and lead our church into financial victory through faith and obedience to God's Word.

Notice how the entire dream came in the form of a parable and was filled with symbols: our church campus, the elderly Ken Hagin, receiving an inheritance, and receiving the offering. The symbols were not too difficult to understand, and the timing of the dream was obviously connected to our current problem. Ken Hagin has also stood as an emblem of faith in both mine and Ron's heart for many years because his teachings had helped to shape our foundation.

Let's go back to Proverbs 25:2: "It is the glory of God to conceal a matter, but the glory of kings is to search out a matter." When my husband sought out the meaning of the dream before the Lord, the message came and reinvigorated faith and direction in the heart of my husband. The dream also hinted of a second church campus that would come as an inheritance, something we didn't grasp at the time because we had just lost the option of buying a piece of property for that purpose. After the recession and to our amazement, we were miraculously given a second campus not across the street but across town.

God knows our past, present, and future. He sees it all in one moment. He knows that to move us into our future with Him, He'll have to awaken our hearts today to His great plans for our tomorrow.

We read His timeless encouragement to the disheartened Israelites at the onset of their Babylonian captivity: "'For I know the plans I have for you,' says the LORD. 'They are plans for good and not for disaster, to give you a future and a hope'" (Jeremiah 29:11 NLT).

Did you know the Creator of the universe masterfully wrote His individualized intentions for every person on the earth before we ever existed? King David gave a description for this: "You saw me before I was born. Every day of my life was recorded in your book. Every moment was laid out before a single day had passed" (Psalm 139:16 NLT). I had read this verse many times, believing it was metaphorical and not literal, that is until I was taken up to heaven by an angel and shown a massive library of books that detailed everyone's life on earth. Those ancient novels are full of living blueprints written by God Himself, our histories recorded before time began. I'll need to clarify that even though God wrote His plans for us beforehand, we still have a free will. We have to be exposed to His plans and then choose to lay hold of them by faith if they are going to happen.

Still, God weaves His plans into the substance of our dreams at night because our waking minds can find them too difficult to believe or they are different from our opinions. His plans might contradict our training or education, they might not be what we want to happen, or they are completely impossible. We read in the book of Isaiah, "For as the heavens are higher than the earth, so are My ways higher than your ways, and My thoughts than your thoughts" (Isaiah 55:9). God's thoughts are not our thoughts, and His ways are not our ways. Through dreams, He can bypass our internal constraints and invite us to rise up and experience His thoughts and ways for our lives. He wants to get His plans—the best plans—across to us. Only He doesn't reduce them to our logic or even our rational language but speaks to us using His language.

We see this process unfold in the life of the patriarch Abraham. God spoke to him about his future offspring and posterity long before he had any. He also sealed Abraham's faith for what seemed to be an impossible future inside his dreams:

Now when the sun was going down, a deep sleep fell upon Abram; and behold, horror and great darkness fell upon him. Then He said to Abram: "Know certainly that your descendants will be strangers in a land that is not theirs, and will serve them, and they will afflict them four hundred years. And also the nation whom they serve I will judge; afterward they shall come out with great possessions. Now as for you, you shall go to your fathers in peace; you shall be buried at a good old age. But in the fourth generation they shall return here, for the iniquity of the Amorites is not yet complete."

Genesis 15:12–16

These plans were already in the heart of God before time began, but they still had to be unveiled to the heart and mind of Abraham before he could cooperate with them. At the direct word of the Lord and through a covenantal dream, Abraham was beautifully led into his future.

Dreams Are Usually Not Straightforward

It's not only prophets who have dreams from God. Over twenty dreams recorded in the Bible were sourced to prophets, kings, and a variety of others. For example, in Genesis 20:1–7, King Abimelech was warned by God in a dream that Sarah was Abraham's wife and not to be sexually intimate with her. At Abraham's suggestion, the king had believed her to be his sister and put her in his harem in ignorance. In Genesis 28:12–17, the patriarch Jacob dreamed of a ladder erected between heaven and earth with angels ascending and descending upon it. In the dream, God reiterated His covenantal promises to Jacob, and he woke up proclaiming the place to be the house of God and the gate of heaven.

The night before Gideon assaulted the Midianite army, Gideon caught two Midianites conversing about a dream one of them had. He dreamed a loaf of barley had rolled into camp and overturned a tent. The Midianite even knew what the dream meant and told his companion, "This is nothing else but the sword of Gideon the son of Joash, a man of Israel! Into his hand God has delivered Midian and the whole camp" (Judges 7:14). In Daniel chapters 2 and 4,

61

King Nebuchadnezzar had shocking dreams about the future, only he needed an interpreter and proof that the interpretation was real and not conjured. The prophet Daniel acquired the details of the dream from God Himself and then provided the interpretation, a feat that earned him a high position in the kingdom. In Matthew 2, we also read about Joseph (Mary's husband) and the Magi who visited the young Jesus. They all received specific warning dreams that served to protect Jesus from being murdered by His political enemies.

Some of the dreams in the Bible were clearly understood while others came in a symbolic narrative and needed interpretation. You will experience this as well. On occasion, you will have a dream that is crystal clear and requires little effort on your part to understand. The majority of your dreams, however, will not arrive in a straightforward narrative. They will involve various scenes and metaphorical sequences, sometimes with words, numbers, colors, places, people, and dialogues. These dreams are not literal but a mixture of symbols deposited into your dreams by the Holy Spirit that hold meaning and direction for your life. Only you'll have to search out the meanings in order to lay hold of the treasure given to you in the night. It's wonderful when someone is around who can accurately interpret our dreams, but with the right building blocks, you too can begin to interpret your own dreams.

• KINGDOM PRINCIPLES •

1. God's thoughts are not our thoughts, and His ways are not our ways (Isaiah 55:8). Through dreams, He can bypass our internal constraints and invite us to rise up and experience His thoughts and ways for our lives.

2. Some of the dreams in the Bible were clearly understood while others came in a symbolic narrative and needed interpretation. You will experience this as well.

3. The majority of your dreams will involve various scenes and metaphorical sequences, sometimes with words, numbers, colors, places, people, and dialogues.

4. These dreams are not literal but a mixture of symbols deposited into your dreams by the Holy Spirit that hold meaning and direction for your life.

5. You'll have to search out the meanings in order to lay hold of the treasure given to you in the night (Proverbs 25:2).

• THOUGHTS FOR REFLECTION •

1. Have you ever received pivotal instruction from God in a dream? Did you understand it instantly, or did you have to search out the meaning?

2. Have you ever broken through personal restraints in life because you saw it in a dream first?

3. How often do you have literal dreams?

4. Does the symbolism in your dreams confuse or frustrate you?

5. Have you considered that dream symbols mean many different things to your life, only you'll have to search that out?

FOUR

Who Is the Dream About?

The first question you need to resolve when you have a dream is to determine who the dream is about. Most of the time, the dream is about you, even if other people are somehow involved in the dream. You are the main action character, and those who appear in the dream may represent an area of your life. Many different people appear in my dreams, and when they do, I ask myself, "What is my relationship with that person?" If they are a friend, then the dream might point to something about friendship. Are they a leader? Then the dream might point to something about leadership. What are their strengths or weaknesses? Or what are their personal attributes that I need to pay attention to? The Holy Spirit might be encouraging me to assimilate these positive attributes into my own walk with Him.

During the first summer of the pandemic, I dreamed that two crocodiles and a crazy man came after me and my husband. I don't recall any more details, but this simple dream contained a volume of information. First of all, the dream was an alert that multiple attacks were coming to target our ministry at the church. That's why my husband was in the dream. You may recall, during that season, nearly every pastor in America came under scrutiny and persecution for either staying open as a church or for closing down, for endorsing face masks or rejecting them, for being politically right or politically left. The crocodiles represented the spirit of Leviathan, which is biblically the spirit king of pride.[1] Job 41 describes it in detail, starting out by asking, "Can you draw out Leviathan with a hook?" and ending with "He beholds every high thing. . . . he is king over all the children of pride" (vv. 1, 34). And the crazy man? That didn't need too much examination as it seemed as if nearly everyone had gone mad—fear-crazy during that time.

What then should you do with a dream like that? When the Holy Spirit gives you a dream, He is speaking to you. When He speaks to you, you need to respond. Don't ignore the dream.

With that, I simply acknowledged the dream and thanked the Holy Spirit for His well-timed alert. Then I prayed according to Isaiah 54:17. "In the name of Jesus, there is no weapon formed against my husband and I or this ministry that will prosper. Any tongue that rises up against us, we will condemn." In my heart, I knew the remedy was to pray out this simple prayer with authority but then keep a posture of humility and not get baited into strife with anyone. (However, that was much easier said than done.)

When You Are the Observer

You will also have dreams that are not about you where you appear in the dream as an observer. You'll have these kinds of dreams much less frequently in comparison to dreams that are about you. Realize there is a right way and a wrong way to handle observer dreams. You might observe a positive or negative situation that involves a person or a group of people, and it will usually be people that you already know. Dreams from the Holy Spirit that involve watching the activities of others are often a call for intercession and, in some cases, a call for encouragement or intervention.

A positive observer dream could be about someone being promoted, being healed, getting married, having a baby, dining at a fancy restaurant, shopping at an upscale store, winning a race, triumphing over an enemy, and loads of other different scenarios. These kinds of dreams could be literal, but most of the time, they are metaphorical.

Your response to the dream is to pray in agreement with what the Holy Spirit has shown you is on the horizon for that individual or group of people, but you'll first need clarity about the symbolism.

A dream where you observe a pregnant person or someone having a baby, for example, might be about a literal pregnancy in their future, but most likely, it is about them coming into a new birth in ministry, a new relationship, a new business or fresh creativity in their business, or something else new. In the Bible, God is always doing a new thing (Isaiah 43:19), and you've been given fresh insight into it.

A simple prayer could be, "Heavenly Father, I thank you for new birth in the life of this person. Let your will be done, let new birth come! In Jesus's name!" In Matthew 6:9–10, Jesus taught us to pray for His kingdom to come and His will to be done on earth as it is in heaven. In other words, by His own design, His will has to be invited into earth's realm through prayer, or His will does not happen.

Dreams are one vehicle through which He communicates His perfect will to us. When you have a positive dream about someone and after you've prayed in agreement, consider that He might have you share the encouraging dream with them. Don't presume this, but you should probably share a dream that is encouraging overall.[2]

When you have a negative dream about someone, it requires a redemptive heart that's equipped with the knowledge of His Bible promises. For example, if you see a person having an accident or dying in a dream and you discern that the dream is pointing to the possibility of a literal accident or untimely death, then you would engage a simple prayer of binding and loosing based on Matthew 16:19 and repeated in Matthew 18:18. "And I will give you the keys of the kingdom of heaven, and whatever you bind on earth will be bound in heaven, and whatever you loose on earth will be loosed in heaven" (Matthew 16:19).

When we bind something, we are tying it up, and we accomplish that by speaking a command (Mark 11:23–24). If I had a warning dream like this about someone, I would say out loud, "In the name of Jesus, I forbid accidents and early death! Thank You, heavenly Father, that You've given Your angels charge over this person, and

You keep them from all harm. I decree that they shall fulfill the number of their days, in Jesus's name!" (See Psalm 121:7; Psalm 91:11; Exodus 23:26.)

The real challenge will be not to tell the person—or anyone else, for that matter—you've had this dream. If you tell them this kind of dream, you could open them up to a foreboding spirit. You'll need to keep most of your negative observer dreams a secret between you and the Holy Spirit. God is revealing His secrets to you and if you can't keep them secret, He will stop telling them to you. You'll also need to learn how to carry a burden like this in prayer without becoming overwhelmed by it. Dreams like this require action in prayer but are not intended to crush you emotionally, something you learn to handle over time in a balanced way.

On the other hand, a dream where you observe someone in an accident or dying could be metaphorical and not literal, but it will still require your intercession. Observing accidents, crashes, or someone dying in a dream might be pointing to something about to go awry or die out in a relationship, in ministry, in their job or business, or in another area of their life. Or they might be experiencing something personal or in their life that feels as if it is about to die, which could be good, bad, or necessary, depending on the context. Again, you will want to seek clarity from the Holy Spirit and pray redemptively as He leads you.

One of my biggest pet peeves when it comes to negative observer dreams is how people handle dreams about leaders, especially ministry leaders, that portray them to be involved in adultery or perversion. After the dream, they blab about it to others, assuming it's true. I have a term for this: prophetic assassination. Prophetic assassination is the act of destroying someone's good character because you saw it in a dream or vision, only there is no tangible proof.

I can't emphasize enough the importance of not sharing negative dreams. The whole point of the dream is to bring the situation to the Lord in redemptive prayer, and in the rare instance that the dream is true, bring the person before the grace of God for conviction of sin and healing. What people don't realize is the Lord really protects His leaders and watches carefully over what He has assigned His leaders to oversee. He will protect His ministers from demonic assignments to steal their moral integrity by alerting someone in a dream about the matter. The dream is intended to trigger the shield of prayer and not slander and gossip. If you ever have such a dream, ask yourself, "What would I want someone to do if they had a dream like this about me?" That should answer your question right there.

Dreams about Those in Your Metron

We know from the Bible that each of us is given a measure, or distribution, of faith and a sphere of authority. The apostle Paul wrote, "We, however, will not boast beyond measure, but within the limits of the sphere which God appointed us—a sphere which especially includes you" (2 Corinthians 10:13). The word for "sphere" in this verse is the Greek word *metron*, which means "measure" or "determined portion."[3] The Holy Spirit will often direct us and speak to us about the people within our metron, and one of the ways He speaks is through dreams.

When you have God-ordained responsibility for someone, either as a minister, a parent, or even as a business owner or employer, a negative dream might lead to more than just intercession. "I dream about my congregants often," said one minister. "The Holy Spirit will often show me in dreams how they are doing in their walk with Him, or He might reveal an area of struggle that needs support and encouragement." He also explained, "Occasionally, I'll observe in a dream when a congregant is doing something that will destroy himself or herself and their family." This minister has learned how to pray and then wisely step in and minister to these kinds of situations. He also keeps his negative dreams in confidence, knowing that dreams from God that reveal sin and vice are not to be uttered. Carelessly voicing them could ruin his credibility as a leader, even if they were proven true.

Years ago, I was leading a mid-week women's group that gathered in the main sanctuary of our downtown Turlock campus. Our gatherings were filled with creativity, connection, food, and laughter. We also worshipped together, and I usually gave a short Bible teaching followed by thoughtful discussion among attendees and prayer. Women came from all walks of life, and most already attended our church, although some were visitors from the surrounding community.

One night after our gathering, I had a dream about two attendees. For some reason, I couldn't see their faces, but I observed that they were in a homosexual relationship. This dream came to me from the Holy Spirit because I was the leader of this gathering, and it was literal and not metaphorical.

The next morning, I invited Him to show me who they were and advise me as to what to do. After a few months, I noticed two new women had joined the group, and they appeared to be friends. They had also begun attending Sunday services. Eventually, both women approached me separately and confessed to their ungodly relationship. They had ended their liaison and truly desired to live a biblically moral life. Although I had a glimpse into the situation already, I was careful to not say anything in public or private. I didn't even hint to anyone in the group that I knew something was going on. These kinds of dreams require wisdom and care, and I trusted the Holy Spirit to bring the situation to the surface in His timing.

Dreams about Famous People

A well-known author and minister was scrolling through one of his social media pages and noticed that someone had tagged him. He clicked on the tag, which had come from a prophet and minister whom he had heard of but had never met. The prophet claimed to have had a dream from God about him and another really well-known person and had shared the dreams on their social media pages. It wasn't a bad dream, only it was very personal and was posted publicly for everyone to read and draw conclusions about.

The author didn't respond to the tag and noticed the prophet had done the same with many ministers and famous people around the globe. When you understand your sphere of authority, then you understand that dreams about people, especially those in spiritual or governmental authority, are not to be shared with the whole world. The minister having the dreams also gave the impression that they had a higher and more special relationship with God, so much so that God would freely share the secrets of others with him. Finally, it implied a relationship between the prophet and the subjects of the dream that really wasn't there. "It would have been much better if the person had sent me the dream privately and not made a big show of it," he said. "Since they didn't, I wrote them off as a person that I could not trust." The prophet didn't understand the boundary lines of their spiritual authority.

Dreams about famous people need to be handled properly. Typically, you don't have any relationship with the person nor do you have spiritual authority over them. For those reasons, you should not share the dream publicly or on social media. One woman posted a video of a prophetic dream about a well-known musical artist. Again, it was very personal and sounded like some kind of prophetic tabloid magazine. I'm not saying the dream was false, but I am saying the dream shouldn't have been made public. Frankly put, when you have a dream about a famous person, it's a call to pray and not to post.

Dreams about well-known ministers, celebrities, or famous people are one type of many common dreams that people have. At times, these kinds of dreams are prophetic in nature and a call for redemptive prayers. Most of the time, however, they are not prophetic. If you dream about a specific actor or actress, for example, the Holy Spirit might want you to look at the roles they play because something about that role is being imparted to you. The same goes with certain ministers. What has God anointed them to do? What are their strong attributes? The Holy Spirit may be nudging you to begin asking Him to anoint you in a similar way.

Once you've determined who the dream is about, the next question you want to answer is if the dream is a positive or a negative one. That might seem overly simplistic, but it will help you to know how to respond.

• KINGDOM PRINCIPLES •

1. Most of the time, your dreams are about you, even if other people are somehow involved in the dream.
2. When the Holy Spirit gives you a dream, He is speaking to you. When you are being spoken to, you need to respond. Don't ignore the dream.
3. You will also have dreams that are not about you, and you will appear in the dream as an observer.
4. Dreams from the Holy Spirit that involve watching the activities of others are often a call for intercession and, in some cases, a call for encouragement or intervention.
5. There is a right way and a wrong way to handle observer dreams. You'll need to keep most of your negative observer dreams a secret between you and the Holy Spirit. You'll need to carry a redemptive heart.

• THOUGHTS FOR REFLECTION •

1. Do you have dreams that are about you but involve other people? Why would the Holy Spirit highlight a particular person in your dream?
2. Do your dreams lead to any meaningful dialogue with the Holy Spirit?
3. If you have a dream that someone is in an accident or dies, should you tell that person? Why or why not?
4. Why is it not appropriate to post dreams about famous people or ministers on social media?
5. How should you handle dreams where you observe infidelity when it comes to others, especially God's ministers?

FIVE

Is It a Good or Bad Dream?

"In tonight's session, I believe you will hear or see the voice of the Holy Spirit and prophesy powerfully to our guests!" We had already soaked the session with prayer, and I said this to encourage the members of my online prophetic community. We were experimenting with a new ministry format that was both exciting and challenging. We had encouraged the members to invite their friends, family, co-workers, neighbors, etc., as guests during our sessions and to receive prophetic ministry from the group. They had mostly targeted those who were unfamiliar with the gift of prophecy and especially those who didn't know Jesus yet. We ended up with all kinds of guests, from hard-core heathens to Spirit-filled pastors. It was very challenging to engage supernatural ministry within this online format, but the results were worth it.

That night, a young woman joined us at the invitation of one of the members. Our session tech granted her entrance into the video discussion from the online waiting room. Participants could view her and me side by side on their screens and post their comments in the rolling thread just below us. As I began the discussion, members began to fire up the chat section with friendly greetings to welcome her. Our guest had intelligent eyes and a caring demeanor and was approximately twenty-five to thirty-five years old. I introduced

73

myself and then invited her to comment. "Welcome to our session today! Please tell us your name and where you are from." She spent a few minutes responding, only I can't remember those details now. Truthfully, I was really buying a few moments of time to hear not only her but also the Holy Spirit on what to do next. I had to quickly figure out how to start moving her and the entire online group into a genuine supernatural interaction.

Soon the members began sharing short prophetic words for her from the Holy Spirit in the thread, words they felt or heard, or images they saw supernaturally just for her. I began to read them out one by one and then periodically checked in with her and invited her feedback. As I did this, I suddenly had a crystal-clear word of knowledge. Words of knowledge are different from prophetic words. Prophetic words in this context will typically exhort and comfort, but they point to the future. A word of knowledge, on the other hand, is a fact shown to you by the Holy Spirit, either present or past, one you couldn't know unless the Holy Spirit showed it to you.

I said to her, "You've had a recurring nightmare that you are being chased." I added, "It's terrified you, and you've had this dream repeatedly." As I spoke this out by the unction of the Holy Spirit, she began to involuntarily rock back and forth in her chair. She lifted her head and seemed to gaze out through her window as she visibly processed the information. The impact of my words coming from the Spirit of God was undeniable. She had just experienced Jesus, the One who knows us intimately and reveals secrets. I invited her feedback, and tears began to flow freely down her face. I finished by saying, "God revealed your recurring nightmare to me because He is at work in your life to dismantle it."

We see from the life and story of the prophet Daniel that God is a revealer of secrets, secrets that may include the dreams of others. "Then the secret was revealed to Daniel in a night vision. So Daniel blessed the God of heaven" (Daniel 2:19). On that day, He chose to reveal her secret to me so she could see Jesus at work in her life, even though she didn't yet know Him personally. It was a bad dream, but one He intended to end.

We will have both good and bad dreams. Bad dreams might steal our peace and need intervention, such as this woman experienced. (I'll address nightmares and sleep disturbances in more detail later in the book.) We will also have a variety of good dreams from the Holy Spirit, which include instructions, wisdom, hints about our future, emotional resolution, healing, a deposit of supernatural gifts, and much more. Again, these dreams will often be metaphorical in nature and come to us as stories and scenes. These dream narratives contain elements we need to examine for understanding and then steward during our waking day with the help of the Holy Spirit.

One woman had a dream during a time she felt overwhelmed with too much anxiety and stress. She dreamed that a "man of light" came up to her and got right in her face. He then pointed a finger at her and said, "I have a word for you. Take it off!" She woke up feeling happy, joyful, and at ease. She knew the dream was from God and was amazed to have the pressure lifted off her in this manner. She enthusiastically described how the dream completely changed the course of her day. "This was one of my favorite dreams," she said. "I felt His love so powerfully."

When it comes to dreams, consider that the Hebrew day doesn't begin at sunrise but at sunset. Many also believe the established times and seasons associated with the Hebrew calendar take precedence over any other calendar.[1] Remember Job 33:15–18, which we read earlier, tells us that, while we are sleeping, God opens our ears, gives us instruction, and does even more. This undergirds the idea that God would begin your day and your new season by actively depositing His perfect plans into your dreams at night.

Does This Explain Déjà Vu Experiences?

Could this be what is really behind a common experience known as *déjà vu*? "Déjà vu" is a French loanword expressing the feeling that one has lived through the current situation before.[2] Many medical and psychological explanations exist for this phenomenon, although most of these are negative and infer you are mentally frail or ill. I've never thought the experience to have a psychological or medical explanation behind it but believed it to be a reflection of some kind of alignment with God. A déjà vu is like walking into a memory only you don't remember ever having done that. I believe it's a waking experience of something you've already dreamed about from the Lord, only you just didn't remember the dream.

To explain this a little better, a woman dreamed that she was sitting with me in a beautiful, peaceful place, and we were dialoguing. My husband arrived at our location in a clean black car. He rolled down the window and shouted, "Are you coming?" She had a second dream like the first, only my husband arrived in a black limousine. He opened the door and shouted, "Get in! It's time to go." Soon after the dream, she and her husband were invited to assist my husband as traveling intercessors. As my husband traveled back and forth to the campuses on Sundays, this couple often joined him in his car and prayed for him. In this case, she remembered the dream upon the outcome.

If this were a déjà vu experience, however, she wouldn't have remembered the dream. Upon entering my husband's vehicle in this manner, she would have entered the experience, though. She would have had a distinct feeling that she had done that somewhere before. Her spirit would have recognized the alignment even if her mind couldn't place it. That's because a scene from her future had already been deposited into her during the night.

Discerning the Source of the Dream

Discerning the source of your dreams will help you know how to respond to them. Typically, three sources are behind your dreams: God, Satan, or your flesh or soul. The source of some dreams can be fairly obvious, but others are not so obvious. For that reason, you'll need to learn the basic identifiers of each source but also have the Holy Spirit's gift of discerning of spirits to sort it out. I wrote extensively about the gift of discerning of spirits in my book *Seeing the Supernatural*, which is about the supernatural ability to distinguish the spirit of the matter, whether it is divine, demonic, or human.

Dreams from God are usually lifting, healing, peaceful, prophetic, or problem-solving, and they might impart gifts and abilities. Some say that dreams from God are brighter and generally more colorful and to look for color to help you source the dream. That can be true for certain people, only that's more of a guide and not a rule. Abraham had a dream that was clearly from God, only it came to him as more of a nightmare. "Now when the sun was going down, a deep sleep fell upon Abram; and behold, horror and great darkness fell upon him. Then He said to Abram: 'Know certainly that your descendants will be strangers in a land that is not theirs, and will serve them, and they will afflict them four hundred years'" (Genesis 15:12–13). Colorful dreams probably are from God but, looking through my dream journal, the color wasn't what told me the source. It was the themes, symbols, and overall tone of the dreams that helped me determine if God was the source. I want to write down these dreams and bring them to God in prayer.

Dreams from God can also include the appearance of His angels. Angels might show up in your dreams, appearing as random strangers, usually in pairs, and help you with a variety of things. The Bible describes how angels have been sent to help us, and they will also help us inside our dreams. "Are not all angels ministering spirits sent to serve those who will inherit salvation?" (Hebrews 1:14 NIV). Occasionally, an angel might speak a message from God in the dream. An angel alerted Joseph, the husband of Mary, in his dreams when the child, Jesus, was in danger and told Joseph where to go to protect Jesus. If an angel gives you a message in a dream, we are exhorted to test the message for congruency with the written Word of God. If the message is directional (i.e., "Sell your home and move to another nation"), you should definitely seek wise counsel before acting on that message.

Dreams from Satan or his demons are typically foreboding and fearful, scenes of death and destruction, prophetically deceitful, or sinful. Upon waking, you might feel absorbed with negative or vain emotional distractions because of the dream. It might open you up to a spirit of fear or deception. It might lure your mind to focus on dark things or false narratives instead of worshiping God. These dreams are sent to try to steal your day, dim your hopes for a good future, or get you to ponder activities that God has condemned. They can be dark and dreary in their overall color and tone. They can feel confusing or draining.

Demonic beings might attempt to speak to you in your dreams by posing as an angel of light, which is a demon pretending to be an angel or God. "And no wonder! For Satan himself transforms himself into an angel of light" (2 Corinthians 11:14). They might use deceptive words, only these words don't align to the written Word or reflect the heart of our heavenly Father. We reject these dreams and don't give them any credibility or place in our lives. We invite the Holy Spirit to come and uproot any demonic seed that might have been planted in our hearts through these dreams and trust Him to instantly remove it.

Sometimes, issues within our own flesh and soul will show up as dreams at night. If you are physically hungry when you go to sleep, you might dream about eating a giant pizza. If you have a strong crush on someone, your crush will probably appear in your dreams. This kind of dream can be emotionally confusing if you don't discern it for what it is. This is not a literal dream but an emotional one. If you are frustrated, you might dream out that topic at night, which is a way to release trapped emotions.

On the other hand, when your heart needs healing, those un-healed issues can show up as persistent themes in your dreams. For example, you might repeatedly dream that you are using the toilet or taking a shower. This specific dream and the repetition of it could be about cleansing or getting rid of something in your soul: anger, lust, unforgiveness, or another sin. When this happens, you'll need to invite the Holy Spirit to come and reveal and heal any unhealed areas of your soul that are demanding attention.

Receive the Gift of Discerning of Spirits

During the height of the pandemic, I had a dream with four main points to it. I was especially careful about discerning the source of my dreams during that season because a plethora of misinformation and chaos was everywhere. This created a blanketing atmosphere over the nation and impacted the dream life of most people that I knew. People were having futuristic dreams that were apocalyptic and sinisterly political, and some even believed their dreams came from the Holy Spirit. These dreams were not prophetic, however, but mostly a form of emotional processing.

This dream came the night before a Sunday morning service. Like I said, it had four main points, only I discerned that just one point out of the four came from Him. I was very grateful that I could sort that out with so much environmental and spiritual noise all around us. The one fact that I discerned as from the Holy Spirit was the name of a woman who would be attending our church the next day. I clearly saw her name in the dream and knew in my heart which service she would attend and where she would be seated. I didn't know her personally, but God did, and He showed her to me in the dream. Armed with that information, I called her out by name that Sunday and gave her a prophetic word, which she confirmed was spot-on.

To sort out this dream, I needed the supernatural operation of the discerning of spirits, which is one of the nine supernatural gifts of the Holy Spirit listed in 1 Corinthians 12:7–10. I want to encourage you that before you go any further with dream interpretation, you, too, will need this supernatural gift if you don't already have it. The gift of discerning of spirits is the supernatural ability from the Holy Spirit to distinguish between spirits—divine, demonic, and human. It also enables us to know the hidden motives of the heart.

I received this gift after I was delivered from a spirit of sorcery during my first year of college, only I didn't know I had it. It's a highly sensory gift, and you will receive information from the Holy Spirit through your senses. You'll see, hear, smell, taste, or feel something, and when you don't know you have this gift in operation, you will mistakenly think that point of discernment is you. Hebrews 5:14 tells us, "But solid food is for the mature, who because of practice have their senses trained to distinguish between good and evil" (NASB). For example, you'll be feeling perfectly fine until someone with mental problems sits next to you, and then suddenly you feel as if you are losing your mind. It takes some practice, but over time, you will learn how to recognize what is you and what is not you and also what to do with the information that you discern. Amazingly, you'll also be able to distinguish the source of your dreams, and this gift will keep you from getting confused.

Does this inspire you to receive the gift of discerning of spirits or a stronger form of it? If so, the Holy Spirit is eager to impart a fresh anointing to you right now. Just put your hand over your heart and pray this prayer to Him:

> *Holy Spirit, You have taught us to pursue love and to desire Your spiritual gifts. You also said that if we ask anything in the name of Jesus, we will receive what we ask for. I deeply desire Your gift, the gift of discerning of spirits, and I want this to grow stronger in me. I ask You to anoint me for this now and thank You for a new and greater ability to discern.* (1 Corinthians 14:1; John 16:24).

Try not to rush away from this moment. Let these words sink in as you tune in to the anointing of the Holy Spirit as it comes upon you. Take some time to bask in His presence, worshiping Him and thanking Him for your new anointing.

With the gift of discerning of spirits in operation, you will notice a difference in how you sort through your dreams. Once you've discerned the source and determined if it's a good or a bad dream, the next task is to examine the content. For some, dreams seem to come as short headlines while others dream in entire novels. Or you might experience a mixture of both. If your dreams are more like headlines, you are not being short-changed. These dreams can surprisingly contain a volume of information once you know how to interpret them. Dreams that seem to go on and on and are filled with endless details might frustrate you and feel like too much information to sort through. When it comes to these kinds of dreams, you won't interpret every detail. You'll want to narrow down the dream's contents to just three or four main points.

• KINGDOM PRINCIPLES •

1. When it comes to dreams, consider that the Hebrew day doesn't begin at sunrise but at sunset. This undergirds the idea that God would begin your day and your new season by actively depositing His perfect plans into your dreams at night (Job 33:15–18).

2. Déjà vu is a French loanword expressing the feeling that one has lived through the present situation before. It's a waking experience with something you've already dreamed about from the Lord, only you just didn't remember the dream.

3. Discerning the source of your dreams will help you know how to respond to the dream. There are typically three sources behind your dreams: God, Satan, or your flesh or soul.

4. Dreams from God are usually lifting, healing, peaceful, prophetic, and problem-solving, and they might impart gifts and abilities.

5. Dreams from Satan or his demons are typically foreboding and fearful, scenes of death and destruction, prophetically deceitful, or sinful.

• THOUGHTS FOR REFLECTION •

1. Do you have more good dreams or more bad dreams? What makes them good? What makes them bad?

2. Are you able to discern the source of your dreams? If so, how?

3. Have you ever had a déjà vu experience? Is it possible it was something you had dreamed before, only you don't remember it?

4. Have you ever encountered an angel in a dream?

5. Have you ever become confused or misdirected as a result of a dream? How did you get back on track?

SIX

Determine the Main Points
of the Dream

The prophet Daniel had a variety of intense dreams and visions about the future. He processed them by writing down only the main facts. We read, "In the first year of Belshazzar king of Babylon, Daniel had a dream and visions of his head while on his bed. Then he wrote down the dream, telling the main facts" (Daniel 7:1). If you follow the details of his dream, he describes the contents for another thirteen verses. That tells me the original dream could have been the length of a short book if he had written it all down. Either way, Daniel gave us a model to follow. When it comes to our dreams, we need to write down only the main points. Why?

Dreams come to us as night parables. When Jesus explained the meaning of the parables in the Bible, He scaled them down to a simple explanation. We need to do the same, or we can easily get lost in the forest of the dream's details and miss the point. One woman, a real dreamer and a prophetic one too, sent me a dream for interpretation. It was about three paragraphs and full of little details. I looked it over and asked her, "Out of all these details, what would you say are the top three or four elements in the dream?" We needed to focus on just the main points and then set the rest aside if we were going to arrive at an interpretation.

Dreams can have so many symbols and scenes that you cannot process and interpret them all. These do not contribute to the overall meaning of the dream anyway. Here is a recent dream that I had to support this:

> I dreamed I was in a hotel room with my son. In the dream, he was eight years old. An Australian prophet came over to the room. She was hit by the Holy Spirit and began laughing hysterically and rolling on the floor. I tried to get a room key at the front desk, but the desk guy sent me in the wrong direction.
>
> I had to climb rough terrain and jump in a river to get where I needed to go for the key. I jumped in and was met by a friendly dolphin, only I ended up in a bad place on land. A woman I knew picked me up in her car, and her phone didn't work. I ended up back where I started, once again asking the front-desk guy for a key. A kid was now handling my request, but he didn't give me what I wanted.

This dream has a lot of little details, but the only ones I needed to pay attention to were the driver and the Australian prophet. This dream was about me, but the driver in the dream told me everything. In real life, this woman is a very insecure person. When I saw her in the dream, I realized that insecurity had been driving me, and insecurity wasn't getting me what I wanted. I brought this to the Holy Spirit in prayer, asking Him to heal me in the areas where I was insecure and stuck. The prophet, however, symbolized my calling and ministry in Australia. It was also very clear to me what these words meant: "an Australian prophet came over . . ." After clarifying this in prayer, I felt impressed by the Holy Spirit to invite this woman to come over and minister at one of my US conferences.

What Area of Your Life Is It About?

Again, your dreams are typically about you, and there will often be people in your dreams and a setting or context. Here are a few examples from dreams that people sent into me for interpretation.

These are not the entire dreams, but I listed key points to show people and settings.

1. I was on a ship with two people . . .
2. I was in my childhood home, and my ex-husband appeared . . .
3. A denominational woman came over and began looking through my cupboards . . .
4. I was at a park and talking with two older gentlemen . . .
5. I was in my home, and a woman was talking loudly to me . . .

The people in your dreams might be family members, friends, neighbors, people at your church, people from your past, strangers, famous people, people from your workplace, your employees, ministers that you know, former spouses or boyfriends/girlfriends, your parents, or literally anyone you've ever had contact with. The settings of the dream might be a school or college, your home or another home, your workplace, your church, a specific room of the house, outdoors somewhere, and so much more.

I listed several possibilities that could appear in your dreams, but really, the list is endless. Remember that your dreams are usually not literal and all these listed are metaphors that have meaning, depending on the context of the dream. This leads us back to the question posed as the title of this section, "What area of your life is this about?" Is the dream about your ministry, school, your job or business, a need for healing or restoration, your family, your relationships with others, your relationship with God, an opportunity, or something else? As you begin to hone in on these, the interpretation is on its way.

Remember that dream context is critical to arrive at a proper interpretation. The five random dream settings I just listed above cannot be interpreted without the rest of the dream. Too often, people will ask these kinds of questions: "What does a fish in my dream mean?" Or "Why did I dream about my grandmother?"

There is no way I can give you an interpretation unless you give me the entire dream. The meanings of symbols will shift depending on the entire backdrop or context of the dream.

Does Your Dream Repeat?

You might have noticed that some of the dreams I've referred to seem to have a repeating element to them. Have you ever had a repetitive dream or dreams with repetitive themes? I received a dream from a pastor, one that he described as a dream within a dream. He said that I had appeared to him in the inner dream and handed him a handbook to break word curses and witchcraft. Next, he saw a person who had been friends with his wife at one time, only they had a falling out. In the inner dream, he watched as the former friend cursed his wife and their marriage out of anger and spite. He came out of the inner dream and then entered the second dream layer. While there, he broke the word curse off his wife and off their marriage.

When he woke up that morning, he leaned over to his wife and inquired about the details. She confirmed that what he had dreamed was accurate, which meant this was a literal dream and not a metaphorical one. He then proceeded to do what he saw himself do in the dream. He broke the word curse, meaning he verbalized a short statement or two in the form of a command to neutralize the impact of her supernaturally charged words against his wife and their marriage. The Holy Spirit is always watching over us and defusing the attempts of the enemy to put us into captivity. He sees what is in the dark and reveals it so we can take action.

I asked him, "What does a dream within a dream mean to you?" He responded that it was a signal to him to pay attention. He felt that the dream within a dream was actually a repeating kind of dream, even though it came as one dream. We see a principle in the Bible that undergirds the purpose of dreams coming to us multiple times. When our good or bad dreams repeat, it's a signal to pay attention. We need to identify and respond to this.

We read that the apostle Peter fell into a trance during a time of prayer on a housetop. A trance is a kind of vision where you lose contact with your natural surroundings and enter another reality by the power of the Holy Spirit. In the trance, he saw heaven opened and several wild animals and birds, things not permissible for him to eat, according to Jewish standards. Yet he was being told to "Rise, Peter; kill and eat" (Acts 10:13). He protested this but saw the image and received the same instruction three consecutive times because the Holy Spirit was preparing him to preach the gospel to a man named Cornelius (see Acts 10). Cornelius was a Roman centurion, but most importantly, he was not Jewish. This was a pivotal moment for Peter and all the apostles and Jewish converts to Christianity. The barrier between Jews and Gentiles had been removed, and Peter was being prepared to begin uniting them together in Christ.

A principle in the Bible refers to establishing things based on two or three witnesses. We read in 2 Corinthians 13:1, "This will be the third time I am coming to you. 'By the mouth of two or three witnesses every word shall be established.'" Although the context is different, Paul was referring to a principle established in the law "at the mouth of two witnesses, or at the mouth of three witnesses, shall the matter be established" (Deuteronomy 19:15 KJV). We also see this principle utilized in several other contexts, for example, in how we deal with conflict and matters of spiritual discipline:

> Moreover if your brother sins against you, go and tell him his fault between you and him alone. If he hears you, you have gained your brother. But if he will not hear, take with you one or two more, that "by the mouth of two or three witnesses every word may be established." And if he refuses to hear them, tell it to the church. But if he refuses even to hear the church, let him be to you like a heathen and a tax collector.
>
> Matthew 18:15–17

We also see it again in connection with prayer:

> Assuredly, I say to you, whatever you bind on earth will be bound in heaven, and whatever you loose on earth will be loosed in heaven. Again I say to you that if two of you agree on earth concerning anything that they ask, it will be done for them by My Father in

heaven. For where two or three are gathered together in My name, I am there in the midst of them.

Matthew 18:18–20

I think you are getting the picture. Here are four basic considerations for repeating dreams:

1. Something has happened or is happening that needs to be addressed.
2. Something is going to change.
3. Satan is attempting to establish something evil and wicked in your life.
4. God is initiating and establishing a blessing in your life.

Very simply, when a dream or elements in your dreams repeat, we need to pay attention. We need to seek the Lord for clarity and a plan of action, or we need to use our spiritual authority to prevent something that Satan is planning, or we need to align with God to receive a coming blessing.

For a season, I began to have a series of dreams. A few elements kept repeating through the series of dreams, and that's why I knew it was important and that I needed to pay attention. I kept dreaming that I was getting on different flights to various countries. These dreams were centered around my calling as a prophet and intercessor to the nations, only repeating issues kept occurring. I either didn't make it on the flight, or the flight didn't take off. I was also consistently losing my wallet, my phone, or my backpack. By the way, wallets, phones, backpacks, etc., are usually symbols that represent personal identity, and I was clearly losing mine in these dreams. The topic of those persistent themes in dreams that I mentioned earlier also applies here.

These dreams and themes were from God. He was warning me not to lose my true identity in Christ. In response, my prayer was consistent. "God, I identify as your child, your daughter, and I am a prophet to the nations. Where I believe a lie about my identity, show

88

me the truth. Help me overcome this clear challenge and attack over who I really am in You." That was a rough season of my life, but I'm glad to say that I did not lose my personal identity or sense of calling in Christ. I'm grateful to report that my dreams finally shifted. I stopped losing these items in dreams but actually found them instead.

Whether your dreams come in the form of night parables or are more literal, the dream world and the spiritual world are much more enmeshed than we've realized. In the next section, I'll discuss different kinds of supernatural dreams and awaken your spirit to the most unusual realm of the miraculous.

• KINGDOM PRINCIPLES •

1. A key to interpreting your dream is to determine what area of your life the dream is about.
2. The prophet Daniel tells us what to do with long, detailed dreams. We need to write them down but only note the main points.
3. Dreams come to us as night parables. When Jesus explained the meaning of the parables in the Bible, He scaled them down to a simple explanation. We need to do the same.
4. Dream context is critical to arrive at a proper interpretation. Symbols in the dream do not stand alone, as their meanings will shift depending on the entire backdrop or context of the dream.
5. When a dream or elements in your dreams repeat, we need to pay attention. Something needs to be addressed.

• THOUGHTS FOR REFLECTION •

1. Are your dreams short and to the point or long with several scenes and activities? For longer dreams, do you struggle to find just the main points?

89

2. Do you have dreams or dream elements that repeat? Why do you think they are repeating?

3. Have you ever experienced a dream within a dream? Does this chapter provide more clarity about why you dreamed that way?

4. Do you have a dream journal? Are you writing down your dreams?

5. Have you noticed that the meanings of symbols in your dreams change, depending on the context and backdrop of the dream?

• DREAM INTERPRETATION APPLICATION •

A woman sent this dream to me:

> My best friend and I were at a self-storage facility, specifically in one of the storage units. The unit was very large with tall brick walls and looked antiquated inside. One of the walls had a gigantic air conditioning vent on it. That vent took up almost the entire wall. My friend and I stood on the opposite side of the room from the vent. We also had a team of movers who had moved all of our belongings out of the unit. Now we could see how huge the room and the air vent were and experience a much cooler room now that it wasn't full of our stuff. I could see water dripping inside the air vent in between the slats. I walked to an upper level of the unit and saw the sleeping quarters for our team of movers and their families. This area had dark-blue carpet. In the dream, their job was finished as everything had been moved out.

Using the building blocks for interpretation, let's break down the dream:

1. Who is the dream about?
    The dream is about her. She is not an observer in the dream.

2. Is this a good or a bad dream?
    It is a good dream.

3. Who is the source of the dream?

    This dream came from the Holy Spirit.

4. What are the main points of the dream?

    The main points are her best friend, the storage room, the air conditioner, and the movers.

5. What area of life is the dream about?

    Her dream coincided with a decision to take an online course in inner healing and deliverance for personal growth. Both she and her friend planned to take it together.

6. Does the dream repeat?

    The dream and the elements of the dream did not repeat.

• INTERPRETATION •

When your best friend appears in your dream, it can represent several things. In this dream, it appeared to be a reflection of an earlier decision that the woman and her friend made together, specifically to take an online course that would deal with matters of the heart for the purpose of transformation. When your best friend appears in your dream, it can also represent a relationship that is safe, familiar, and a confidential place to share your secrets. Dreaming of your best friend might also be about Jesus. The Bible describes Jesus as the Friend that sticks closer than a brother (Proverbs 18:24). Based on the narrative and the metaphors, this wonderful dream was authored by the Holy Spirit and was showing the dreamer what was going to happen.

The storage unit appeared old and cluttered, which caused the unit to be stuffy and overheated. Given the backdrop of her recent decision, the storage unit appeared to symbolize her heart, specifically that her heart had stored away a lot of old things that needed to be cleaned up and cleared out. We are reminded of the proverb, "Keep your heart with all diligence, for out of it spring the issues of life" (Proverbs 4:23). On another note, the unit was large, which probably meant that she was largely compassionate and big-hearted toward others.

The air conditioner produced a refreshing wind blowing through the storage unit. In this context, the air conditioner was a symbol for the Holy Spirit. The Bible describes the Holy Spirit as coming like a wind to us at times. (See Ezekiel 37:9–10; John 3:8; John 20:22; Acts 2:2.) In the dream, He was sending His refreshing winds to her and blowing upon her heart. She would experience the full, cooling effect of His refreshing winds, however, once she got things out of her heart that were in the way.

Who were the movers in the dream? These were probably angels sent to help her through the heart-excavation process. Angels have been sent to help all of us. They also strengthen us in hard times. (See Luke 22:43; Hebrews 1:14.) These angels were positioned to remain with her for as long as the process required.

There were a few other miscellaneous details, specifically the dripping water and the dark-blue carpet, which might have been an illustration of a body of water. These symbols were pointing to the refreshing waters of the Holy Spirit and maybe a few other things. These elements were just extra dream information that could be looked at more closely for encouragement if needed. In any case, the Holy Spirit was all over this dream and communicating this woman's future. She was being prepared for a powerful move of God within her own heart.

• INTERPRET YOUR DREAM •

Write your dream here:

Using the building blocks for interpretation, break down your dream:

1. Who is the dream about?

2. Is this a good or a bad dream?

3. Who is the source of the dream?

4. What are the main points of the dream?

5. What area of your life is the dream about?

6. Does the dream repeat?

• INTERPRETATION •

1. Ask the Holy Spirit to direct your heart toward His interpretation of the dream.

2. Take some time to study the possible meanings of the symbols from your main points section using your Bible and/or a Christian dream symbol dictionary for the symbols not in the Bible. What do you think these three or four symbols represent? Where does your heart rest after you've examined the possible meanings?

    a.

    b.

    c.

    d.

3. After looking over the building blocks and also the meanings of the symbols, what appears to be the overall gist of the dream?

4. How does the meaning of your dream lead you to pray or take action?

DREAMS ARE A GATEWAY TO THE SUPERNATURAL

SEVEN

You'll Connect to the Spiritual Realm in Dreams

Some say that dreams act as a portal to the supernatural. Keep in mind that I am using the term "portal" very loosely, only because some people think it is a New Age term.[1] A more general definition for the word *portal* would be "gate" or "entrance."[2] I've wondered about the connection between our dreams and the spiritual realm for years, even before I became a Christian. When I was a young teenager, I was sharing about the prophetic dreams I was having with a Mormon bishop. I didn't use the term "prophetic," but that's what kind of dreams they were. My dreams were mostly about me with one about a specific natural disaster, and all these dreams came to pass. Mormons have a foundational theology that includes encounters with the supernatural. Keep in mind that they believe in a different Jesus than Christians do and have erroneously scribed sacred books to supplement the Bible.[3] For that reason, my comments to the bishop were not shut down or dismissed, only we didn't credit them to God out of ignorance.

The patriarch Jacob had a dream one night where he saw a ladder erected between heaven and earth, and angels were ascending and descending upon the ladder. The Lord stood above the ladder and spoke out His promises to him in the dream, causing Jacob, upon waking, to believe he had found the gate of heaven (Genesis 28:10–17). This dream provides us with a picture that describes the heaven-to-earth connection that often transpires in dreams. Dreams are a gateway to the supernatural, and you will have various spiritual encounters in your dreams, both positive and negative. For that reason, I have added some needed teaching points throughout this section in order to maintain balance and congruency with the written Word.

One hot summer night, I fell asleep and began to dream. I was acutely aware of the voice of the Lord throughout the night. In what felt like a long and continuous dream, I heard the first and last name of a woman repeatedly. I also dreamed repeatedly about a Scripture in connection with her. "And whatever their sickness or disease, or if they were demon possessed or epileptic or paralyzed—he healed them all" (Matthew 4:24 NLT).

I woke up feeling strangely connected to the information because the Holy Spirit's power was all over it, only I wasn't sure who this woman was. I checked my church rosters and my online group rosters and could not locate anyone with this name. All I knew to do was to post a request on my social media asking if anyone knew her and, if so, to email my ministry or send me a private message. A small group of people tagged a woman with that specific name in the thread. She had been in one of my online groups in the past, only I had forgotten who she was since I equip thousands of people online. She responded to my inquiry by posting to her social media page that she had experienced issues with her heart and had just seen her cardiologist. He had given her a clean bill of health even though she had many alarming symptoms. She concluded, "The night Jennifer Eivaz received the word and spoke it out over me, that very day my blood pressure suddenly went down. All the heart palpitations, heartburn, weariness, and headaches ceased."

Whether it's hearing the random names of people in our sleep, seeing numbers, events, and/or dates, or interacting with people in our dreams in a variety of ways, our dream narratives often contain underlying supernatural elements. For example, I was looking through my dream journal for the past three years and noticed how many of my dreams carried strands of information that revealed the future. These small pieces of information were tucked inside the general storylines of the prophetic dreams and came to pass. I didn't know these bite-size pieces of information were prophetic in nature until after they happened. I'm so glad I wrote the dreams down.

If you keep a dream journal, look through your dreams over a period and see if you notice any similar patterns. If you don't have a dream journal, I encourage you to begin one today. Dreams, even the ones we don't understand, need to be written down and examined for information. Your crazy dreams can be surprisingly rich with information once you break down the symbols. If you don't write down your dreams, you'll most likely forget them, as most dreams seem to quickly vanish from our memories. I'm in the habit of writing down my dreams. I've even found dreams that I wrote out in the middle of the night but forgot about until I reviewed my dreams several weeks later.

Are Lucid Dreams Actually Spiritual Dreams?

I was studying the nature of lucid dreams and drew the conclusion that these dreams, although codified by sleep researchers, are way more spiritual than we've realized. By standard definition, a lucid dream is a type of dream in which the dreamer becomes aware that they are dreaming. During a lucid dream, the dreamer may gain some amount of control over the dream characters, narrative, or environment; however, this is not actually necessary for a dream to be described as lucid. Neuroscientists have a few theories for why people have lucid dreams, but the true cause has remained largely unresolved.[4]

We see several instances of lucid dreaming in the Bible. In the book of 1 Kings, we read how King Solomon had just offered to God one thousand sacrifices at the great high place in Gibeon. In response to his offerings, God met Solomon in a dream that night and said, "Ask! What shall I give you?" (1 Kings 3:5). Solomon responded, "Give your servant a discerning heart to govern your people and to distinguish between right and wrong" (1 Kings 3:9 NIV). His response pleased the heart of God, and he was rewarded with great wisdom, wealth, and fame. Solomon's dream appeared interactive. He was able to think and respond to the voice of God inside his dream. It was a lucid dream and definitely a spiritual one.

Not only might we encounter God or His angels in this kind of dream, but unfortunately, we might encounter darker aspects of the spiritual realm. For example, I've interviewed several women who've had past relationships with highly occult men only to have these men appear in their dreams at night to bother and sexually harass them. They've all shared that the dreams were lucid in nature, and these men were entering their dreams through magic. For that reason, they've had to learn to take control of the dreams as they were happening, something much easier said than done.

Interestingly, most have shared how they've not yet been able to completely stop these dreams from happening, which speaks to the level of spiritual binding between the individuals.[5] Keep in mind that these dreams were not symbolic but more like a virtual reality experience. I should mention that having a dream about a former relationship is not automatically a lucid dream. When it's lucid, you are aware in the dream that you are dreaming, and you might have some control over the dream narrative. A non-lucid dream involving an ex-relationship can symbolize several things, however. Depending on the context of the dream, it could be a warning from the Lord not to go back to something in your past.

Satan Will Target a Nation of Dreamers

During my initial research for this book, a word from the Holy Spirit dropped into my heart, and it was simply to research the dream life of Fijians of all things. I've never been to Fiji and don't know anyone of that nationality, only I came across a fascinating thesis paper regarding their dream life.[6] This particular paper was written in the 1980s and targeted a small segment of the population for dreams research on the island of Fulaga, a small raised limestone island in Southern Lau Province, Fiji. The author and researcher provided a glimpse of how their dreams and the spiritual realm intersect:

The morning after my arrival in the village that was to become my home for the next 19 months, the chief, in whose house I was staying, initiated my language instruction. "Ko seg ani tadra ni bogi?" This was translated by his daughter to mean, "Did you dream last night?" My heart leapt since I had a long-standing interest in dreams. I could hardly believe my good fortune in unknowingly landing in a field site with people whose first greeting of the day was to inquire into the dream experiences of the preceding night. I launched into an enthusiastic rendering of the night's dreams, but his face stiffened and he and others stared off in what I later learned to be a clear expression of embarrassment. Only months later, as the intricacies of the language became more clear, did I recognize the double negative in the question—"You did not dream last night?" The "correct" answer is "yes," meaning essentially, "yes, I slept well, I was not bothered by any dreams."[7]

According to Barbara Herr, Fijians believe their dreams to be real experiences, that visions and dreams are the same and just separated by light and dark or awake and sleep, and their dreams are given to frequent encounters with spirits. They believe in soul departure and the reality of encountering other beings in the dream state, such as ancestors, the spirits of other living persons, as well as other good or nefarious spirits. This belief and experience were so strong that when one man murdered another and ran into the forest to hide, nobody went looking for him to bring him to justice. They knew he probably wouldn't live through the night due to the terror of the forest spirits. As expected, he was found dead a few days later, supposedly from terror.

With the introduction of Christianity and the instruction that all such spirits were devils, they were taught to pray for dreamless sleep. This was to prevent them from entering a demon-possessed state of dreaming. This instruction not only denied their culture but denied a clear realm of expression that originated in God. It would have been better to teach the Fijians how to discern the spirits and spiritual warfare, rather than attempt to shut down their dreams.

Just reading between the lines and given my understanding of the spiritual realm, I recognize when Satan has strategically targeted a group of people and why. This tribe, and probably the entire Fijian nation, is most likely full of prophetic seers who are collectively wired by God to see into the spiritual realm. Various tribes and people groups actually carry this as a generational blessing in their bloodline. Without salvation through Jesus and the power of the Holy Spirit, what God intends to be a blessing becomes a curse instead. Satan and his demons came in to target their seer gift and make it as dark and terrifying as possible. This tells me this tribe's strongest expression lies within the contents of their dreams. Once they've submitted their supernatural gift to the written Word of God and the Holy Spirit, they will terrify the entire demonic order by what they dream at night. Much like the not-yet-Christian Indigenous Australian, the Fijian's dream world needs to be purified but not denied.

There are myriads of different supernatural dream expressions. In the next chapters, I will describe the most common categories of supernatural dreams in anticipation that you've experienced one or more. I also know the power of testimony. We read, "For the testimony of Jesus is the spirit of prophecy" (Revelation 19:10). In other words, when you hear or read a testimony, it functions like a prophetic word. It has the power to reproduce in you. Reading these chapters is going to awaken an anointing for dreams of like kind and more in your life.

• KINGDOM PRINCIPLES •

1. Dreams are a gateway to the supernatural, and you will have various spiritual encounters in your dreams, both positive and negative.
2. Whether it's hearing the random names of people in our sleep, seeing numbers, events, and/or dates, or interacting with people in our dreams in various ways, our dream narratives often contain underlying supernatural elements.
3. Dreams, even the ones we don't understand, need to be written down and examined for information. Your crazy

dreams can be surprisingly rich with information once you break down the symbols.

4. Lucid dreams, although codified by sleep researchers, are way more spiritual than we've realized. In a lucid dream, the dreamer becomes aware that they are dreaming while dreaming. They may gain some amount of control over the dream characters, narrative, or environment; however, this is not actually necessary for a dream to be described as lucid.

5. Various tribes and people groups carry the propensity for visions and dreams as a generational blessing in their bloodline. Without salvation through Jesus and the power of the Holy Spirit, what God intends to be a blessing becomes a curse instead. Satan and his demons will come in to target their gift and make it as dark and terrifying as possible.

• THOUGHTS FOR REFLECTION •

1. Have you experienced a supernatural dream before? Was it positive or negative?

2. Overall, have you noticed a prophetic quality attached to your dreams?

3. Have you ever had a lucid dream before? What was the source of your dream?

4. Do you come from a bloodline that is generally blessed to have visions and dreams? Can you see the importance of being in right relationship with Jesus when it comes to that kind of gift?

5. Have you been instructed to deny dreams and the supernatural because you might encounter demons? If so, what are your thoughts now after reading this chapter?

EIGHT

God Protects You through Warning Dreams

A mother in Southern California dreamed that it was raining really hard outside and her oldest son was driving with her grandson in the back of his vehicle. In the dream, her son drove through an intersection at the green light and was T-boned by another vehicle on the side where her grandson was sitting. She woke up from the dream, startled and praying strongly in her prayer language. Later that day, she arrived at work and noticed that it had been raining hard all day, much like she saw in her dream. She was also praying throughout the day because the dream wouldn't leave her.

She arrived at a patient's home and began to work on them when her phone rang. Normally, she didn't answer phone calls when she was with her patients. But it was her son, the one who was in her dream. Because of the dream, however, she knew to answer the phone. Sure enough, her son had called to tell her he had been in a car accident. His car had spun out of control on the freeway and hit a wall. Although he totaled the car, he miraculously walked away uninjured. She asked him, "Where's my grandson?" He replied that her grandson would have been with him, only he and his mother got into a disagreement right before he left, and she and their son stayed home.

When God gives you a warning dream, it's not to make you afraid. You are being given inside information from the Holy Spirit so you can act on that knowledge and get the best possible outcome. This mother woke up from the warning dream praying in spiritual tongues for the protection of her family. Something about the dream engaged her spirit. She was also impressed by the Holy Spirit to keep praying throughout the day. The dream, followed by her prayers, changed what would have been a terrible outcome and saved her family from death.

We see several examples of warning dreams in the Bible. The Lord, by His very nature, is our shield and very fierce protector. "After these things the word of the LORD came to Abram in a vision, saying, 'Do not be afraid, Abram. I am your shield, your exceedingly great reward'" (Genesis 15:1); "The LORD will fight for you, and you shall hold your peace" (Exodus 14:14).

He will even send warning dreams to people who don't know Him yet as their Lord and Savior. For example, Pontius Pilate served as the governor of the Roman province of Judea and was the official who presided over the trial of Jesus. His wife, who was not a believer in Jesus, had a dream right before her husband condemned Jesus to die. As Pilate sat on the judgment seat, she sent a message to him, saying, "Have nothing to do with that just Man, for I have suffered many things today in a dream because of Him" (Matthew 27:19).

Her dream confirmed what Pilate secretly thought about the unjust charges that had brought Jesus before him for trial. This further motivated him to try to free Him from execution. Pilate continued to rationalize for His release with the chief priests and elders, to no avail. He tried again by presenting a ludicrous option to them that allowed him to either release Jesus or a notorious murderer from prison. They chose to release the murderer while fiercely insisting that Jesus be crucified. To stop a violent riot from erupting, Pilate reluctantly ordered His death.

Warning dreams will come to us from God's protective nature to keep us aligned to His plans for us. We should never be afraid when we have a warning dream. Think about the clear warning dreams that encompassed the birth and early years of Jesus. The wise men from the East arrived in Jerusalem searching for Jesus, the King of the Jews, because they saw His star appear in the sky. When they inquired of His whereabouts, King Herod invited them to search out His location but to report back to him when they found Him. They did find Jesus but were warned in a dream not to return to the king, a decision that infuriated the ruler.

Next we read, "Now when they [the wise men] had departed, behold, an angel of the Lord appeared to Joseph in a dream, saying, 'Arise, take the young Child and His mother, flee to Egypt, and stay there until I bring you word; for Herod will seek the young Child to destroy Him'" (Matthew 2:13). Joseph fled with his family to Egypt and narrowly escaped Herod's order to murder all the male babies and toddlers two years old and under who were living in Bethlehem.

Later, Joseph was informed in another dream to go back to Israel. "Arise, take the young Child and His mother, and go to the land of Israel, for those who sought the young Child's life are dead" (Matthew 2:20). Joseph took his family back to Israel but was afraid to return to Bethlehem, knowing that Herod's son Archelaus was now ruling Judea.[1] He was warned again in a dream and instructed to go to Nazareth and reside in Galilee instead. All these were in fulfillment of prophecy about Jesus.[2] "When Israel was a child, I loved him, And out of Egypt I called My son" (Hosea 11:1).

We will have dreams from God that show us both where we need to go and where we don't need to go. All these dreams are to keep us aligned to God's plans and purposes for our lives.

Once I dreamed in detail about a middle-aged woman with vibrant red hair who lived in a specific city of the United States. I didn't know this woman in real life, but I knew that she hated me and wanted nothing good to come my way. Was this dream literal? Spiritual? I wasn't sure. It happened to be one of those dreams that sticks with you after you wake up, though, only I didn't understand why. I wrote it down and forgot about it.

Around three months later, I woke up one morning with that dream strongly on my mind. Later in the day, I checked my emails and noticed a ministry request had come in for a women's event. I didn't know the coordinator who had invited me, but I did notice another minister had already been confirmed to speak. I investigated her online and was shocked when I saw her photo. She looked just like the red-haired woman in the dream! I checked into her a little further. Not only did she look like the woman, but she also resided in the specific city that I saw in the dream. Needless to say, I didn't accept the ministry invitation and was very grateful to God for giving me that warning dream.

You might have a single warning dream from the Lord, or you might have a warning dream multiple times, or a warning theme might show up across multiple dreams. A single warning dream, even if it feels heavy and engages your spirit, can most likely be averted or the impact lessened through your simple intercession. Multiple warning dreams are a clarion call to immediately come before God in prayer over the outcome of the dream.

This happened to a friend of mine right before her pastor betrayed her and her husband. She saw her pastor in various narratives over a series of dreams, and the dream symbols all pointed to some kind of betrayal. The dream came this way because it was established and couldn't be avoided. God gave her these dreams to prepare her heart ahead of time, and she began to intercede by asking the Lord for the most redemptive outcome possible.

As you know, this level of betrayal can deeply wound people and take them out of their race. That didn't happen to this couple, however. Because of the dreams, they leaned into God for strength and grace to navigate the situation once it happened. Instead of retreating with hurt and bitterness, they soared in ministry instead. Make sure to pray about what you've been dreaming. This puts God in control of the outcome and brings His protective shield over your heart and life as well.

Identifying False Warning Dreams

Everything that God does, Satan will attempt to counterfeit. He will attempt to bring false warning dreams and even repetitive warning dreams. How, then, do you know the difference between a warning dream from God and a false warning dream from Satan? Remember that God often deposits His plans for your future into your dreams at night. That deposit can be likened to the planting of a seed in your heart and is intended to produce a specific harvest later. Satan is trying to mimic this activity. He's trying to make his own deposit and establish something deceptive and destructive in your life. You might experience a series of repeating dreams, for example, that something bad is going to happen to you, such as an accident or a dream of your spouse leaving you or that your child goes missing or dies. These dreams can be accompanied by a choking fear or a sense of total helplessness or hopelessness.

Whenever you have a warning dream, it's important to first discern the source of the dream so you know how to respond. When you are aware of God's heart and His promises from continual study of His written Word, you will easily identify the counterfeit because it doesn't align with what you know about God. You'll recognize that your dream doesn't look, sound, or feel like Him. One of my baseline Scriptures to help me discern properly is, "The thief does not come except to steal, and to kill, and to destroy. I have come that they may have life, and that they may have it more abundantly" (John 10:10). When I see unwarranted death, theft, and destruction to my future in my dreams, then the dream is most likely from Satan and not God.

Our response to a false warning dream is to first harness any wild and negative emotions that may have come with the dream. If you falsely dream that your spouse has abandoned you, then you'll need to take care not to punish them verbally or emotionally for something that happened in a dream. Dreams like this might engage deep insecurities and require personal discipline to hold those emotions in submission to the Holy Spirit. Secondly, do not give voice to the contents of the dream. Satan has supplied you with a narrative and wants you to negatively engage your faith by saying what he is saying and not what God is saying.

We read, "Death and life are in the power of the tongue and those who love it will eat its fruit" (Proverbs 18:21). Satan knows these

Scriptures too and will attempt to twist these spiritual laws against you but only if you let him. Next, find a clear promise of God in the Bible to counter that negative dream and begin to give voice to those promises instead. When I've had dreams concerning the well-being of my children, I never give voice to the dream. I habitually begin to decree from Psalm 91 that the Lord is our refuge and no evil befalls us.

Warning dreams will lead us into some kind of intercession almost every single time. That might happen right as you wake up when the dream is fresh on your mind, or you might continue praying for a day or more until you feel the burden of the dream has lifted. Sometimes, you'll find yourself praying and interceding for yourself and others while you are actually dreaming. I would describe this as an extension of a warning dream, only it's not just a dream but an intercessory dream. You really are praying for the matter, and this kind of dream can be unusually intense.

• KINGDOM PRINCIPLES •

1. When God gives you a warning dream, it's not to make you afraid. You are being given inside information from the Holy Spirit so you can act on that knowledge and get the very best outcome.

2. Warning dreams will come to us from God's protective nature and to keep us aligned to His plans for us.

3. A single warning dream, even if it feels heavy and engages your spirit, can most likely be averted or lessened in impact through your simple intercession.

4. Multiple warning dreams are a clarion call to immediately come before God in prayer over the outcome of the dream.

5. Make sure to pray about what you've been dreaming about. This puts God in control of the outcome and brings His protective shield over your heart and life as well.

• THOUGHTS FOR REFLECTION •

1. Have you ever had a warning dream before? What was the outcome?

2. Have warning dreams in the past caused you to be afraid? Do you now understand why God gives warning dreams?

3. Have you ever had a false warning dream? How did you know it was false?

4. Warning dreams can engage deep emotions and insecurities. Have you experienced this?

5. Have warning dreams ever led you into deeper dialogue with God? Did you find a sense of release or peace afterward?

NINE

Powerful Intercessory Dreams

"During the summer of 2020, I had a very vivid dream about a meeting with my church's lead pastor at his office desk," a woman shared. "In the dream, I explained who I was in Christ and who I refused to be in order to please people or conform to the church's expectation." She added that she communicated these things very humbly and lovingly, although she was firm and sincere. She knew the dream was significant and kept praying into the theme of the dream for months afterward. She presumed the dream was about her and thought she might be heading into a conflict with her pastor.

That following year, her pastor had considered leaving due to the overwhelming pressure to adapt his convictions to please his congregants. Only he didn't do that. Instead, he chose to dig deep into his true heart of loving people and helping them to develop and mature as believers in Christ. In hindsight, she figured out this was an intercessory dream on his behalf. The dream came abstractly, but this is the nature of dream language.

God masterfully intervened in the life of her pastor by allowing her to "stand in the gap" in her dream as if she were the pastor making the difficult decision. Standing in the gap for something or someone is an act of intercession that gains God's attention. In

Ezekiel 22:30, we read the words of the Lord, "I looked for someone among them who would build up the wall and stand before me in the gap on behalf of the land so I would not have to destroy it, but I found no one" (NIV). The illustration used in this verse is that of a wall with a gap or hole in it. An enemy can break in wherever there is a gap or breach in the city wall. The gap has to be repaired as soon as possible, but until then, it needs to be swarmed by militant defenders.

Intercessory dreams are dreams where you are positioned powerfully by the Holy Spirit to stand in the gap. In these kinds of dreams, you will most often see, feel, and experience yourself interceding or praying inside your dream. You might be praying for yourself, and you really *are* praying even though it is happening in a dream. More often, you are praying for someone else or praying for an entity, such as a church, school, government building, business, etc. You also might see yourself praying for a geographical location, such as a city, region, or nation. Many people who've experienced an intercessory dream will say it can be exhausting, as intercession inside your dreams carries an unusual intensity.

Jesus Continually Prays for Us

Jesus is our great High Priest and Intercessor. The writer of Hebrews tells us about the power of His blood sacrifice and resurrection. "Therefore He is also able to save to the uttermost those who come to God through Him, since He always lives to make intercession for them" (Hebrews 7:25). This means that you and I are being prayed for continuously. When Jesus overturned the tables of the money changers in the temple, He shouted out their violation for all to hear. "And He said to them, 'It is written, "My house shall be called a house of prayer," but you have made it a den of thieves'" (Matthew 21:13). They had violated the prophecy that described the modern-day church as a house of prayer for all nations. "For My house shall be called a house of prayer for all nations" (Isaiah 56:7). Jesus insists that His church engage in continuous intercession on the earth.

The definition of *intercession* in the Bible is a "prayer, petition, or entreaty in favor of another."[1] When Jesus taught the disciples about prayer at their request, He taught them that, by God's design, nothing happens in the earth unless a person petitions God for it. He said, "In this manner, therefore, pray. . . . Your kingdom come. Your will be done on earth as it is in heaven" (Matthew 6:9–10). This is a powerful and sobering thought because we typically don't consider ourselves to have this much authority or influence with God. Nevertheless, without an intercessor, His will on earth is simply not done. I firmly believe, however, that He stirs up prayer in the hearts of His people wherever and whenever needed. He will also bring forth powerful and continual intercession through us inside our dreams.

"I had a dream and saw a large group of angels in front of me," said a woman from my online mentoring group. "Jesus stood with me and told me to release the angels into Afghanistan. He said, 'You are releasing ministering spirits for my remnant.'" In the dream, she lifted up her hands and began to pray and worship Jesus. As she did that, a large portal opened wide between heaven and earth, and the angels poured through. She looked to her right, and other intercessors had their arms raised and were doing the same. "I was suddenly in the nation of Afghanistan," she further described with wonder. "I was escorted into a room filled with women, and they all had heavy chains on their ankles. I prayed for them in the dream in my prayer language, and the chains began to loosen."

Imagine that! Desperate women on the other side of the world who probably believed they had been forgotten in their deep affliction. God sees and knows the suffering of mankind. He doesn't overlook anyone. He will raise up an army of intercessors all over the earth to pray for His will to be done, and He will release effectual prayer in dreams.

Spiritual Warfare and Intercession in Dreams

The apostle Paul described our present warfare. He wrote, "For we do not wrestle against flesh and blood, but against principalities, against powers, against the rulers of the darkness of this age, against spiritual hosts of wickedness in the heavenly places" (Ephesians 6:12). Intercessory dreams may involve spiritual warfare against demonic beings over the souls of men, either directly or indirectly. This is what makes these dreams so intense.

A young woman described her intercessory dream and the miraculous outcome. She dreamed she had walked into a room with walls made of cement blocks. She saw her brother weeping while seated on the edge of the bed when an angel suddenly appeared. She began comforting her brother while praying powerfully in her prayer language. Demons were trying to come into the room, but the angel fought them off. She told her brother they couldn't stay in the room and they needed to worship their way out, and that was the end of the dream. For context, she explained that she and her brother had a terrible argument and had not spoken with each other for years. He also suffered from PTSD from his time in the military. A few weeks after her dream, remarkably they began talking again, and their relationship was miraculously restored.

I've had many such intercessory and spiritual warfare dreams, largely because I'm a prophet and intercessor to the nations. These kinds of dreams usually reflect the specific spiritual battle for geographical areas or for matters impacting the nations in general.

Around September 2022, I was dreaming off and on through the night and heard these words being repeated over me, "You are a champion." Then I saw a large and hideously ugly giant as it was being led into an open arena packed with excited spectators. You could tell the giant had not seen any light for some time as he squinted in pain under the bright lights of the arena. He was led to the center of the arena by a thick neck chain attached to a collar with a link on it. I knew in the dream that these kinds of demonic beings did not have names and liked to stay very hidden. The Voice, which was the Holy Spirit, asked me to name him. My response was "Name him Extreme Darkness." With that, Extreme Darkness was led away from the arena for his judgment and total destruction. The dream was unusually intense, and I woke up from this dream exhausted.

To provide the backdrop, I had been instructing throughout 2021 about "rulers of darkness" and how they were going to be exposed. The Holy Spirit had been revealing this to me, only I didn't know why. I had explained to my social media audience that we had focused much of our intercession and spiritual warfare upon the powers and principalities, but we had overlooked this classification of beings listed right alongside them in Ephesians 6:12.

Rulers of darkness operate in the following manner:

1. They masterfully hide themselves.
2. They are the spirit agents behind every cover-up.
3. They keep sinister schemes hidden and in the dark.
4. They blind and bind people into silence on many levels.
5. They are the spirit agents behind every sinister secret network and organization.
6. They fiercely resist and deny exposure.

It was an unusual revelation when I received it, but circumstances unfolded throughout the nations that seemed to support what I had been hearing from the Holy Spirit. I was also praying into this alongside my intercessory teams, specifically that God would pour out His glory in the nations and these demonic rulers of darkness would become bound and exposed. The dream about the giant was an intercessory dream and perhaps a conclusion to the prayer journey that I had been on for over a year.

When God gave Adam dominion over all creatures, He granted him the right to name them. Naming the creatures implied dominion and authority. When Jesus ran into the demoniac in Mark 5, He asked it to name itself. When Legion replied, Jesus cast out the legion of demons. When I was asked to name the giant in the dream, I was being positioned by the Holy Spirit to use my spiritual authority and exercise dominion. In this case, I just needed to name the creature. In this context, naming him was the equivalent of defeating him, so he was then led out for judgment.

Let the high praises of God be in their mouth,
And a two-edged sword in their hand,
To execute vengeance on the nations,
And punishments on the peoples;
To bind their kings with chains,
And their nobles with fetters of iron;
To execute on them the written judgment—
This honor have all His saints.
Praise the Lord!

Psalm 149:6–9

Dreams that involve powers and principalities and, in my case, rulers of darkness can be very intense dreams. Things first happen in the spiritual realm and then in our natural realm as a result of these kinds of dreams. I've discovered that some of these dreams can also lead to tangible financial breakthrough.

◦ KINGDOM PRINCIPLES ◦

1. Intercessory dreams are dreams where you are positioned powerfully by the Holy Spirit to stand in the gap.

2. When you have an intercessory dream, you will most often see, feel, and experience yourself interceding or praying inside your dream.

3. Many people who've experienced an intercessory dream will say it can be exhausting, as intercession inside your dreams carries an unusual intensity.

4. God sees and knows the suffering of mankind. He will raise up an army of intercessors all over the earth to pray for His will to be done. He will cause effectual prayer to happen in dreams.

5. Intercessory dreams may involve spiritual warfare against demonic beings over the souls of men, either directly or indirectly.

• THOUGHTS FOR REFLECTION •

1. Have you ever had an intercessory dream? Did you know you were actually praying?

2. Have dreams like this ever exhausted you? If so, how did you recover?

3. Have you ever interceded in a dream for another nation or people group? If so, was that a one-time dream or a repeating dream theme?

4. Have your intercessory dreams ever involved direct spiritual warfare?

5. Do you notice a heightened connection to the spiritual realm after having any form of an intercessory dream?

TEN

Miracle Provision Dreams

A friend of mine dreamed that a male acquaintance had given her a blank check to purchase items for a wedding. The backdrop of the dream was about going to a wedding, but the focus of it was really about the blank check. Around eight months later, the person in the dream reached out to her and gave her a check for $1,000. He found out she had started her own ministry and wanted to bless her with a financial gift.

Soon after receiving the check, she had another dream. In this dream, she held several envelopes full of money but had laid them down somewhere in order to take care of something. When she went back to retrieve the envelopes, they were all gone. Now panicking, she reached out to a friend for help and recovered all the envelopes except for one. In the dream, the Holy Spirit told her she would recover her lost money and, specifically, $30,000. Something miraculous began to awaken in her life right after she had this dream. People were being led by the Holy Spirit to give her random amounts of cash, ranging from a few hundred dollars to $1,000. She was then offered random jobs she could easily manage from her computer at home. She also received an unusual stream of miracle income, something that only God could have provided.

All Money Has a Spirit on It

There is a surprisingly supernatural side to finances that many of us are not aware of. Dreams like my friend had are not too common, and they are deeply spiritual. I believe God wants to awaken our faith and also our dreams to unlock even more miracle provision in our lives. This leads us to a question posed by Pastor Robert Morris, senior pastor of Gateway Church in Dallas/Fort Worth. He asked, "Did you know that all money has a spirit on it?"[1] He goes on to explain that money either has the Spirit of God or the spirit of mammon on it. Money in and of itself is neutral, but when it is submitted to God and used for kingdom purposes, the Spirit of God is on it. This money is shielded from the devourer and has the capacity to supernaturally multiply.

Money that isn't submitted to God and His purposes will have the spirit of mammon on it by default. Mammon, also known as the god of wealth, is an ancient Assyrian deity that demands total worship and will not let you worship God with your resources. There are variations of this deity from culture to culture, but it behaves the same. Jesus acknowledged this truth when He taught, "No one can serve two masters; for either he will hate the one and love the other, or else he will be loyal to the one and despise the other. You cannot serve God and mammon" (Matthew 6:24). Mammon seeks to convince you not to obey the Lord in the giving of tithes and also to withhold your offerings from the house of God. It seeks to blind you with greed, choke you with debt, and rule you through a deep fear of scarcity. When you know how spiritual money really is, you will better understand the miracle nature of provision dreams and awaken to the possibility of receiving them.

A woman shared a miracle provision dream that came to her while attending one of my conferences at Harvest Church. She dreamed she was at the conference during a time of transition between two sessions. She said that I came and sat behind her and began talking to the women who were also seated behind her. She turned around in her seat to face all of us and to listen to the conversations. When she did that, I pointed at her in the dream and shouted, "Financial breakthrough!" She then turned to the right and the left, trying to determine who I was really talking to because she didn't think it was her. When she turned back to look at me, I said again emphatically, "Yes, I'm talking to you! Financial breakthrough!"

At the time of the dream, she and her husband owned their own business, and it had been very hard on them financially. They had found themselves unable to keep up. After her dream, they experienced an immediate financial breakthrough. They received a job for about $20,000 and then another for about $11,000 when they normally did jobs for around $3,000. They were so encouraged by this, and their faith in God's provision grew as a result of this experience. Ultimately, they sold their business and were led by the Holy Spirit to move to Turlock. She's now a pastor on our staff, which might have been the reason that her dream took place during a transition.

He Is Jehovah-Jireh, Even in Dreams

Jehovah-Jireh is one of the many different names of God found in the Old Testament. Jehovah-Jireh or *Yahweh-Yireh* means "The LORD will provide" (Genesis 22:14). This was the name of the location where Yahweh told Abraham to sacrifice his son Isaac as a burnt offering. Abraham chose the name when God provided the ram to be sacrificed in place of his son Isaac. We learn from this illustration that we can obey God in returning the tithes and giving our offerings because He is our source and supplier. God gives us a prescription to receive His provision. He said, "Give, and it will be given to you: good measure, pressed down, shaken together, and running over will be put into your bosom. For with the same measure that you use, it will be measured back to you" (Luke 6:38). We obey the Lord by returning the tithes because the tithes belong to Him and by also giving our offerings. He determines how abundant provision emerges in our lives, but it will come. It will be supernatural, and it might come through a miracle provision dream.

For a season, I had a series of intercessory and spiritual-warfare dreams for the state of California. The dreams were mostly about the safety and future of children, and I was battling with a Jezebel spirit. The Jezebel spirit is a very real demonic principality that was first mentioned in the book of 1 Kings and later in the book of Revelation. This spirit being is highly perverse and the demonic force behind the destruction of marriage as an institution, traditional family, and the innocence of children, among other things. I have a much deeper teaching about this spirit principality and how to set people free from it in two of my books, *Seeing the Supernatural* and the *Inner Healing and Deliverance Handbook*. My dreams during that season were highly contentious and occurred just before a series of bizarre laws came into the state that targeted traditional marriage, the safety and sexuality of children, and the safety of the unborn.

In one of those dreams, I was holding a small, fluffy white dog in my arms. I wrote a threatening note to Jezebel and then attached it to the dog's collar. The note read, "I am coming after you." I then directed the dog to go to her palace off in the distance and to find her. I watched from a distance as she gleefully gathered the darling little pup in her arms but then found my note and read it. She became visibly furious upon reading my words and immediately broke the neck of the dog in spite. That was the end of the dream, and all those dreams were similarly highly contentious and violent.

During this time, one minister's wife shared an unusual dream with me. She described how I had rebuked a demon and commanded it to come off her finances. She further explained, "You specifically said to the demon, 'I'm coming after you!'" She didn't know about my dream and how this was the exact threat I had made to that Jezebel spirit. She and her husband were also preparing to move to Brazil as full-time missionaries. They desperately needed funding, only it wasn't coming in, and she was concerned. Promptly following her dream, they began receiving significant and multiple donations toward their ministry. It still shocks me to know that a spirit principality on this level was holding her money back. Once it was dealt with through a dream, the floodgates opened.

How often is wealth held back from us by these demonic principalities? The answer, is more often than we think. I was ministering in Florida at a church led by a well-known prophet. The spiritual warfare surrounding this conference was unusually heavy, and I was relieved when the conference was finally over. I had a dream the night after I flew home, which was a Sunday at around 3:00 a.m. The dream was set in the city I had just ministered in, and I went face-to-face with a demon called "chaos." The dream encounter was so real and heavy that when I woke up, I could feel the spiritual contention happening all around me even though I was fully awake.

A few hours later, I was communicating the dream to my husband while we were readying ourselves for church. Right when I told him the details, he received a text message. A woman wanted to know how she and her husband could best donate to our church because the amount was quite large. They also lived in Florida just north of where I had been, which led me to believe that my dream and their gift were somehow connected. I was dealing with a high-level principality from that area, and the contention shook out a financial blessing aimed at our church.

The sad and difficult part of this story involved a man who went into that same city's airport just forty-eight hours after I had flown out. He came to the airport armed with a weapon and shot as many people as he could, killing several. I struggled quite a bit with this because I knew everything was spiritually connected. Should I have prayed more? Why did people have to die? I had a lot of questions about it and sought counsel from another prophet about the matter. I appreciated his words when he said, "God always has multiple people on any one prayer assignment, and more people would have died if you had not prayed at all."

I Decree Wealth-Transfer Dreams

As I wrote this chapter, I began to feel the distinct presence of the Lord specifically on the contents. I'm convinced that God has ordained a new transfer of wealth for those who've been faithful to His instructions about tithes and the offerings. I now decree Job 22:28: "Thou shalt also decree a thing, and it shall be established unto thee: and the light shall shine upon thy ways" (KJV). I decree that the powers and principalities are now being dealt with, the heavens are being shaken, and miracle provision dreams are being awakened at night. My prayer for you is to specifically have these kinds of dreams and to see the miraculous provision of the Lord on a whole new level.

I am always amazed at how God works powerful financial miracles through this realm of dreams. Principalities and powers, even rulers of darkness, are being dealt with, resulting in wealth being released back to His church. Not only does He cause miracle provision through dreams, but He also powerfully heals and delivers people.

• KINGDOM PRINCIPLES •

1. There is a surprisingly supernatural side to finances that many of us are not aware of.
2. Jehovah-Jireh is one of the many different names of God found in the Old Testament. Jehovah-Jireh or *Yahweh-Yireh* means "The LORD will provide." This is ultimately a supernatural provision.
3. All money has a spirit on it, either the Spirit of God or the spirit of Mammon.
4. Money that isn't submitted to the Spirit of God and His purposes will have the spirit of mammon on it by default.
5. Being faithful in our tithes and offerings releases the Spirit of God on our money, causing it to multiply. Abundant provision might also come as the result of a miracle provision dream.

• THOUGHTS FOR REFLECTION •

1. Have you considered that there is a supernatural side to finances?
2. Do you believe that God is your source of provision?

3. Jesus said plainly that we either serve God or Mammon with our money. Is this challenging to you?

4. Have you ever experienced miracle provision before? Have you experienced it through a dream before?

5. Are you experiencing spiritual warfare for your finances? If so, could higher-level demonic principalities be involved? What is the clearest Biblical strategy to counteract this level of warfare?

ELEVEN

Supernatural Healing Dreams

During an all-church prayer session, I felt impressed by the Holy Spirit to pray and lead others to pray for the health and safety of the babies in our church. I felt this prayer burden for about two weeks, but I don't remember ever praying for just this in all the years that I've led prayer sessions at Harvest Church in Turlock. A prayer burden can feel like a weight pressing upon your person or emotions and usually carries a distinct thought. You are then compelled to pray and keep on praying until the burden lifts. By the way, this prayer burden didn't overwhelm me or interrupt my ability to do life, but it stayed with me for that long.

Toward the end of this time of targeted prayer, a woman at our church gave birth to her first child. Serious health problems emerged, and the baby was put in the Neonatal Intensive Care Unit. The baby's parents and grandparents were all very prayerful people, only they did not know I had been leading prayer in this direction for a few weeks already and didn't know why.

In a dream, the grandmother saw the turnaround. She told me later, "Jennifer, you appeared to me in a dream and told me everything would be okay." She found out the next day that her grandbaby took a turn for the better the very night she had the dream. I am happy to report the child is perfectly healthy today.

Dreams with narratives and outcomes like this are absolutely awesome. At the same time, they could lead to some pretty dangerous questions, such as, "Did you, Jennifer, feel or sense that your spirit had appeared in the grandmother's dream?" Or "Did you send your spirit to her and speak to her in that manner?" I know enough people with this kind of thinking that an experience like this could lead to some highly unbiblical conclusions. I want to assure you that I did none of those things.

It was definitely a healing dream with a strong prophetic edge, but all I did was partner with the Holy Spirit in prayer. He foresaw the problem and created the solution. The Holy Spirit answered this grandmother's prayers for healing through a dream and then chose me as a metaphor to deliver the news. Based on what unfolded and how it was resolved, the illness that struck the baby was definitely a high-level demonic attack. This child has been marked by God for something amazing and was an overcomer from the beginning.

His Healing Knows No Borders

"Throughout the Bible, people have given many names to or for God. Sometimes they were given in response to something God had done; other times, they were to describe who He is."[1] Jehovah-Rapha is a popular and extremely important name for God that means "the God who heals." He healed many people throughout the Old Testament, and when Jesus came to earth, He healed many people and even raised people from the dead. We read this powerful truth: "Jesus Christ is the same yesterday, today, and forever" (Hebrews 13:8). He has not changed and continues to heal today and will continue healing us until we receive our resurrected bodies and no longer need healing anymore.

How many ways does God heal physical bodies? If you look at the numerous verses in the Bible about healing, you'll see that He heals in many different ways. Jesus often touched people, and they were instantly healed, or He merely spoke a word and healing took place. "Then Jesus put out His hand and touched him, saying, 'I am willing; be cleansed.' Immediately his leprosy was cleansed"

(Matthew 8:3). "The centurion answered and said, 'Lord, I am not worthy that You should come under my roof. But only speak a word, and my servant will be healed.' . . . Then Jesus said to the centurion, 'Go your way; and as you have believed, so let it be done for you.' And his servant was healed that same hour" (Matthew 8:8, 13).

In John 9:6, He made clay out of dirt mixed with His own saliva and placed the clay on a blind man's eyes and healed him. (See also Mark 8:23.) In Mark 7:33, He placed His fingers in a man's ears and he was healed and able to both hear and speak. We see how many people were healed in the New Testament just by having faith in the healing power of Christ. (See Luke 17:19.) Even today, people receive healing the same way, by having faith in Jesus the Healer. The Bible instructs us to lay hands on the sick and they will recover and we are also exhorted to anoint sick people with oil and pray the prayer of faith. (See Mark 16:17–18 and James 5:14–15.)

Supernatural healing also comes by the gift of faith, gift of healings, and working of miracles by the empowerment of the Holy Spirit. (See 1 Corinthians 12:9–10.) My point is, healing in Christ is available for us today in a variety of miraculous ways. We have a tendency to put borders around how God can heal us when His healing touch has no borders. Another consideration is that He heals physical bodies in dreams, and He does so more often than we realize.

A man had a fungus on all of his toenails. It was quite unsightly, and he was embarrassed for anyone to see his feet. The nail fungus was so bad that his doctor declined to prescribe any oral or topical medications because he didn't believe anything would cure it. The man had discerned that something about this was more spiritual than physical, and he was praying and standing on God's Word for healing. "I felt shame," he said. "It was as if the devil wanted me to walk around in shame."

In a dream, he saw himself praying for his feet to be healed. A loud shout that sounded like thunder came from the sky. Suddenly, lightning hit both of his feet, and they were healed. When he woke up, he was afraid to look at his feet because the dream felt so real. When he finally looked, he was disappointed because his feet had not changed like he had seen in the dream. But three months later, to his surprise, he noticed the new nails growing in were all healthy. Keep in mind that this man had not taken any medication for the problem. His toenails were miraculously healed, and now he had no more fungus. This healing came from God and happened through a dream.

If God is healing in dreams, is it then possible to become sick in a dream? If you dream that you've become sick in some manner, usually the sickness is symbolic and not literal. Some, however, have experienced spiritual warfare in a dream, the kind that caused sickness to appear in their body.

Dreams of Infirmity Are Usually Symbolic

A ministry wife had a short dream that a serious infection had thickly oozed out of her right thumb. She really didn't have an infection, but the dream felt weighty and something she needed to inquire about and process with the Holy Spirit. When I say the dream felt weighty, what I mean is the dream carried a heavy anointing from the Holy Spirit, the kind that brought attention to the heart and mind of the dreamer.

Using the building blocks for dream interpretation, we can easily narrow down the interpretation of this dream. The dream was about the dreamer, and the main points were her right hand, the thumb, and the infection. The narrative seemed alarming, only the symbols revealed something else: what area of her life the dream was really about and why.

Some believe the digits of the hands represent aspects of the fivefold ministry[2] as outlined in Ephesians 4:11:

1. The thumb represents the apostle. It's the only one that touches all others and is the finger that enables us to grip.
2. The forefinger represents the prophet. This finger points the way, being a corrector and a director and one who unveils the rhema will of God.
3. The middle finger represents the evangelist. It is the farthest reaching.

4. The ring finger represents the pastor. He is married to the sheep and always with them.

5. The pinky represents the teacher. This finger gives balance to the hand.

The dream metaphor of the right hand versus the left hand also holds a distinct meaning. In short, the right hand can symbolize authority, strength, ability, and honor. (See Exodus 15:6; Psalm 89:13; Psalm 45:9; Hebrews 8:1; and Genesis 48:13–19.) It can also mean that something is happening right now or a right thing is happening right now because it's happening on the right side. Conversely, the left hand could symbolize something that is on track to happen, only it's not happening right now. It will happen at a later time.[3]

The ministry wife dreamed about the thumb of her right hand because she was married to an apostle. Her dream revealed a nasty infection leaving the thumb of her hand, which implied something was being healed in her relationship with her husband and it was happening right then. The good news is both she and her husband had been working hard on their emotional health in that season and it was showing up as real growth in their marriage. They knew they needed intentionality in this area in order to have better relationships with each other and also in general. This dream was a confirmation of their progress, despite the repulsive imagery.

Most dreams about infirmity are symbolic and either positive or negative, depending on the context. If you have a dream like this, you can sort through it with the Holy Spirit and by using the building blocks for dream interpretation to arrive at an interpretation. On occasion, people have dreams that lead to an actual physical sickness. If this ever happens to you, you'll need to know how to battle in order to beat it.

Dreams That Cause Actual Sickness

I was ministering at a prophetic conference in New South Wales when the Holy Spirit gave me a prophetic act in connection to

Australia's First Nations people who were present. As I performed the prophetic act, the Holy Spirit suddenly poured out upon the room, resulting in mass travail, healing, and deliverance from demons. He is shockingly good, and that night was unforgettable.

When the conference was over, I immediately noticed a problem with the bottom half of my mouth and chin. They had become numb as if I had been injected with novocaine, making it challenging to both eat and speak. I flew to western Australia and had dinner with the pastors of the church I would be ministering at next. I mentioned the problem, and the pastor associated it with the Maori indigenous group from New Zealand but then clarified that none were residing in his area that he knew of. Apparently, Maori women often display a personalized tattoo on their chin that is deeply significant to their spirituality and culture.

A few days later, in the middle of the night, I was in between that awake and sleepy, dreamy state when I saw a Maori male off in the distance. His eyes were firmly fixed on mine as he shot something at me. I discerned the force of sorcery like a sharp and mighty arrow coming right for me. It struck me straight in the chest, and I woke up instantly ill and unable to get out of bed. I contacted my personal intercessors, who did tremendous battle in prayer on my behalf, and my body began to recover by the next afternoon. It was fully resolved within twenty-four hours, although it felt like forever. This was becoming an unusual spiritual battle, only I didn't know why.

I contacted my personal assistant, who lives in Australia, and told her what happened. She was preparing to fly over for the weekend to assist me as I ministered and informed me that a Maori family was flying in too. She said, "We're not sure why they are coming to the conference. They aren't Christians."

That Sunday, I could feel the spiritual battle all morning as I ministered, only this family was not even present. During the evening session, four Maori women appeared, and the eldest had the traditional chin tattoo. As I began to speak, I publicly honored them and invited them to sit in the front row as I shared my testimony of salvation with everyone. As I continued speaking, the power of the Holy Spirit began to fall upon the room for salvation, causing this family to weep and cry out in repentance. It was a monumental moment and explained why I was dealing with so much spiritual warfare.

I heard the Holy Spirit speak again. "Pray for ears in the room to be healed." I didn't notice until then that one of the Maori women had a hearing device for both of her ears. When I called for the healing for deaf ears, she took off her device because her ears were healed at that very moment.

I'm grateful to God for answering prayer and that sudden sickness that came on me because of a dream cleared up quickly. That's not always the case. If this happens to you, you'll have to go to battle in intercession and make decrees for healing over yourself from the Word of God. I've known a handful of people who've encountered spiritual principalities in dreams and become ill as a result, some for a long time. They've all since received their healing, and some were healed in their dreams. In each case, they had to stand on God's Word for divine health, fight their way through it, and not give up.

He has sent His word and healed you (see Psalm 107:20), and He heals in a variety of ways, including inside our dreams. Salvation in Christ includes our personal salvation from eternal damnation and also our healing and deliverance. *Strong's Concordance* defines the Greek word *sozo* as "to save, heal, preserve, and rescue."[4] Bethel Church in Redding, California, describes it this way:

> The word *sozo* . . . is used over 100 times in the New Testament, especially whenever Jesus heals someone, be it physically, emotionally, or spiritually. *Sozo*, then, is the 'full package' of salvation, healing, and deliverance that Jesus came to give to people!"[5] (See Romans 10:9; Luke 19:10; Matthew 9:22; Luke 8:36.)

He saves you and heals you, even doing so in dreams. In the same way, He will also deliver you from demons. I know countless numbers of people who've been powerfully delivered from spiritual strongholds in their dreams and woken up free.

• KINGDOM PRINCIPLES •

1. Jehovah-Rapha is a popular and extremely important name for God that means, "the God who heals." He healed throughout the Old Testament, and when Jesus came to earth, He healed many people and even raised people from the dead.

2. We read this powerful truth: "Jesus Christ is the same yesterday, today, and forever" (Hebrews 13:8). He has not changed and continues to heal today. He does so in a variety of ways.

3. Most have not considered that He also heals physical bodies in dreams, and He does so more often than we've realized.

4. If you dream that you've become sick in some manner, usually the sickness is symbolic and not literal. Something in your life needs to be repaired or healed.

5. Some have experienced spiritual warfare in a dream, the kind that caused sickness to appear in their body. If this ever happens to you, you'll need to know how to battle in order to beat it.

• THOUGHTS FOR REFLECTION •

1. Have you ever experienced a miracle healing before? Have you ever experienced it through a dream?

2. Are you mindful of balancing supernatural dream experiences with clear biblical parameters?

3. Have you ever dreamed that you were sick in some manner? If so and if the sickness was metaphorical, what was the dream really about?

4. Have you ever become sick as a result of a dream? If so, did you recover?

5. Why might someone have to battle more intensely to come out of a sickness caused by a dream?

TWELVE

Dreams That Bring Deliverance

A common testimony was coming in from people that I knew and even people that I didn't know. Individuals kept claiming I had appeared in one or more of their dreams and had either given them a prophetic word and/or delivered them from a demon. Those who reported being delivered had awakened with no more afflictions and were free from bondage. What was going on? Why did the Holy Spirit choose to use me as a symbol and messenger of deliverance in people's dreams so many times? I've considered a lot of theories, but I think the best possibility behind the phenomenon is that it's the fruit of my intercession.

I am a seer prophet, an intercessor, and a personal and geographical deliverance minister. In other words, I don't just bring deliverance to individuals, but I go after whole regions and tackle strongholds in regions and nations as the Holy Spirit leads. Most of my intercession for people and geographical areas falls along these lines. Perhaps God chose to answer some of my intercession within the realm of dreams. I'm still not completely sure, but without exaggeration, I've heard several thousand such testimonies, and I praise Jesus for every one of them.

A Hispanic Christian business woman shared her powerful dream with me. She said, "On the Fourth of July, Jennifer Eivaz was in my dream. I was in a white bathrobe on a street and getting into a brand-new white Cadillac Escalade. The person who picked me up was an old high school friend named Liliana. She stepped out of the vehicle and yelled, 'In my dream, I saw the word *Ju-le* written above my head. (It was spelled just like that.) I don't understand!' I told her to look up the meaning of the name. Right then, Jennifer showed up and stood on the opposite side of the vehicle to the right. We both turned to see her, and she hollered back, 'I know what it means! Ask me when you wake up from this dream, and I'll tell you!' Jennifer smiled, and Liliana drove off. I was left standing there in a white bathrobe."

Using the building blocks for dream interpretation, let's break down this dream. First of all, this dream was about the dreamer. It was a good dream that came from the Holy Spirit. The main points were the white robe, the new white vehicle, the old friend, and myself. This woman is a powerful seer and intercessor, and her dream occurred on the Fourth of July, which is Independence Day in America, the day we celebrate freedom from oppression. I concluded the date of the dream was significant and not a coincidence because of who she is in the Lord. Most of the symbols in her dream had cultural meanings, but you'll see how the interpretation and the outcome fell in line with the Bible and with the heart of God.

My interpretation to her was this, "You are going to experience an Independence Day! A Day of freedom! The white bathrobe represents robes of righteousness. The Lord is delivering you from the impurity of your past and from generational strongholds. You wore this robe in the dream because you've been washed and are clean and pure (see Revelation 7:14 and 19:14).

"The Cadillac Escalade is a symbol of a high-class vehicle and a favorite of your nationality. Vehicles in dreams often represent ministry as well. You entered a large vehicle, meaning you entered a large ministry and specifically deliverance ministry from everything you've been delivered from. That is why I stood in your dream on the right side of the vehicle because I symbolize deliverance, and your deliverance is happening right now.

"The word *escalade* means "the act of scaling a fortified wall or rampart."[1] The name *Liliana*[2] means purity and the name *Ju-le* (Julie) at one time meant "purity" although the meaning seems to have been adjusted to now mean "youthful." Ju-le might also be a play on words and mean "Jewel." All these names, however, were symbols that reinforced what God is doing in you. You are being delivered, you walk in freedom and purity, and you will minister to others out of your personal deliverance."

Her Response Blew My Mind

I was shocked at what happened to her once she received my inter-pretation. She remarked, "It took me a while to write back to you because after I read your interpretation, I felt that in the following days, there would be some type of manifestation." Her premonition was right, and she described the following weeks afterward as a full-on war. "I felt assured that despite it all, I would come out pure and victorious," she said.

The Holy Spirit began to shine His light on personal strongholds and generational curses in her bloodline. For a few weeks, she was compelled by the Spirit of God to fall on her knees in prayer and face reality. She underwent a deep process of repentance, surrender, crying out, and personal deliverance that was being led by the Holy Spirit and then worship at every new level of freedom.

Strangely, each issue that came up was preceded by a different physical ailment. In repeated studies, science confirms diseases can manifest in the body when the soul is injured through sin or trauma due to the interconnection of the body, soul, and spirit.[3] For exam-ple, she experienced an eye infection, then fever blisters, a urinary tract infection, and then not being able to breathe at night. With each incident, she invited the Holy Spirit to reveal the root of the ailment, and He lovingly and faithfully did so. "I was so taken aback by all of it," she said. "Each ailment was a physical manifestation of generational curses, iniquity, and strongholds."

She went through multiple layers of deliverance but felt the abiding presence of the Holy Spirit the entire time. Each time something came up, He was right there to help her work through it to victory. She went on to experience new freedom that went layers deep inside her. What was amazing is that it all began in a dream.

What Is Deliverance?

An adult male with an overall grudge against the Christian church and anything religious shocked his mother when he asked if she needed help with a conference at her church. She was a faithful churchgoer who served on the security team, and she did need extra manpower. He agreed to help and attended the conference for that purpose.

As he listened to the preaching, he found himself coming under the strong conviction of the Holy Spirit. He sheepishly made his way to the altar, and the power of God came upon him so strongly that he was unable to remain standing. (Second Chronicles 5:14 talks about this. "So that the priests could not stand to minister by reason of the cloud: for the glory of the LORD had filled the house of God" [KJV].) A pastor arrived to find him lying on his back on the floor and shaking strongly under the presence of God.

All of a sudden, something shifted. He began to manifest demonically when a demonic spirit attempted to hold his neck to choke him and cut off his air supply. He could both see and feel, as well as clearly articulate what was happening. The pastor cast out the murderous demon with a simple but repeated command, "Come out of him now! In Jesus's name!" The demon left with a shriek, and the man immediately surrendered his life to Jesus Christ.

When Jesus was on earth, He cast out devils everywhere by the power of the Holy Spirit. We read, "How God anointed Jesus of Nazareth with the Holy Spirit and with power, who went about doing good and healing all who were oppressed by the devil, for God was with Him" (Acts 10:38). These nefarious spirits will afflict humans with sickness, terror, death, and every oppression you can think of. They will drive people to do great and horrific evil wherever and whenever possible.

God's church needs deliverance ministry. Deliverance is casting out demons by the power of the Holy Spirit. Jesus assigned us to deliverance ministry as part of the Great Commission, and we are anointed to preach the gospel and bring freedom from demons in much the same way He did. "And He said to them, 'Go into all the world and preach the gospel to every creature. . . . And these signs will follow those who believe: In My name they will cast out demons" (Mark 16:15, 17). When someone manifests demonically, we command the demon to come out in Jesus's name, and it must go. We see this in Acts 16:18: "But Paul, greatly annoyed, turned and said to the spirit, 'I command you in the name of Jesus Christ to come out of her.' And he came out that very hour."

Keep in mind that a non-Christian is under the power and control of the devil by default until they give their life to Christ. (See Ephesians 2:2.) There is no neutral position in this regard. A person is either ruled by a demonic spirit or the Holy Spirit, depending on their choice of allegiance. A non-Christian might not manifest demonically like this man did when committing their life to Christ, but it can and does happen. Thankfully, this church was prepared for that possibility and able to bring this person through the process successfully.

When a Christian experiences demonic oppression, however, it's not because they are possessed in their human spirit the same way. That's impossible because they are now regenerated into the new birth by the Holy Spirit. (See 1 Corinthians 6:19.) Their oppression is the fruit of some kind of internal agreement with a lie that has partially aligned them to the demonic kingdom. I know several Christian men and women who claim to love Jesus but are immoral, addicted, and lacking integrity. Or they are chronically sick, mentally ill, and can't keep a job or relationships. These are often the fruits of demonic agreements within, and they need to get delivered and rebuild their internal world on the rock of God's Word.

The whole idea that Christians can have spiritual problems is a touchy subject. Many Christians have devastating spiritual problems that will remain unresolved until they can repent and renounce the lie(s) they believe and exchange it for God's truth. Many erroneously believe that Christians cannot exhibit demonic manifestations, especially dramatic ones. When the Holy Spirit in His goodness begins to challenge a demonic agreement within, a demonic manifestation of some kind might occur.

I've known people during an anointed church service to suddenly be unable to breath, get dizzy or nauseous, feel a vise grip clamp down on their head, and more. These are symptoms that something needs to be dealt with, and we need to ask the Holy Spirit what it is. Even so, some lies and demonic agreements are embedded so deeply within that we can't possibly begin to process them in our waking state. For that reason, God might initiate our deliverance within a dream because in that realm, we can't resist His anointing quite as easily. We will experience the powerful results, however, and our lives will change for the better.

Delivered from Ancient Strongholds in Dreams

Not all demonic oppression is the same. Some of it comes because of what is happening within, but other times, it comes because of what is happening in connection to the land we live on. In the introduction, I had mentioned a demonic attack on my breathing right before I went to Australia for the first time. I had unwittingly entered into a spiritual contention with an ancient deity and stronghold revered by many indigenous non-Christians that hosts aspects of a python spirit.

I learned so much from this experience and have conducted targeted deliverance ministry around the globe for the python spirit. As a result, many people diagnosed with asthma, COPD, or other respiratory challenges have been healed after receiving deliverance prayer from this sinister and constricting spirit. I've included those prayers in the appendix section for you to utilize if ever needed. I've also received testimony from those who were delivered from this ancient python in their dreams. Most of them were Australian, which confirmed why it was considered by indigenous to be a "dreamtime" being.

The wife of an Australian man consistently complained that he was always wheezing and insisted that he go to the doctor, only he never did. He crawled into bed one evening, short of breath and wheezing badly. He fell asleep and had a powerful dream. "In the dream, I was at the hair salon, and Jennifer Eivaz was cutting my hair. I told her I was having breathing problems, wheezing, and shortness of breath. As she was cutting my hair, she began to pray strongly for me. She bound a demonic serpent spirit around my chest, and when she finished, my breathing returned to normal and the tightness in my chest left."

He suddenly woke up and realized he had been dreaming. Only his wheezing had stopped, and his chest felt lighter. Since the dream, he no longer uses an asthma inhaler, and his wife hasn't complained about his breathing either.

A woman from Australia also had terrible breathing problems that began in early childhood. She suffered from shortness of breath and had tendencies to get bronchitis, asthma, and other respiratory illnesses. She commonly took asthma medication and steroids just to breathe. She attended one of my conferences in Australia and was ultimately delivered from a python spirit.

"In 2019, Jennifer Eivaz ministered at a conference in Byron Bay, Australia," she explained. "She called people to the front who were experiencing respiratory issues, and two of us went forward. When Jennifer prayed for the other woman, she let out a terrific scream and then slithered on the ground like a serpent. Jennifer assured me that I would not do the same thing and then said, 'You are extremely prophetic.'" Apparently, this woman had experienced the negative side of the prophetic in a previous church, and she despised it. When I gave her that word, she changed her mind, feeling a sense of value, calling, and destiny.

After the conference, she went on vacation with her family and friends. Her asthma was severe because they were in the Australian bush with dirt and campfires, and they were bushwalking to find wombats. That night, she had a dream. "Jennifer Eivaz began to pray for me, and I felt a snake tightly strangling me around my throat. She began to cast a python spirit out of me, but it wouldn't leave. She then handed me a golden key and said I had authority to cast out demons in Jesus's name. In the dream, I commanded the python to leave, and it flew out of my chest."

When she woke up, she didn't reach for her inhaler as she normally would. Since then, she has prophesied, interceded, loudly praised God, and exercised without taking asthmatic medication. She has not had those debilitating asthma attacks and respiratory problems either. "I was delivered from a demon in my dream," she exclaimed. "I also received an anointing from the Holy Spirit to deliver people with similar issues. I am inspired to help others find the freedom I have found."

After hearing so many testimonies like these, I'm convinced that certain bondages will only shift in the realm of dreams. When we are asleep, our defenses are down, and our stubborn logic is suspended. This is the perfect environment for God to act on our behalf and bring new freedom. Unfortunately, our spiritual enemies know this to be true as well. They won't just attempt dark or deceptive dreams, but they will also attempt to create horror-filled dreams and nightmares.

• KINGDOM PRINCIPLES •

1. When Jesus was on the earth, He cast out devils everywhere by the power of the Holy Spirit (Acts 10:38). This is the ministry of deliverance and can also happen within dreams.

2. Nefarious spirits will afflict human beings with sickness, terror, death, and every oppression you can think of. They will drive people to do great and horrific evil wherever and whenever possible. These spirits are empowered by deception and falsehood.

3. Many Christians have devastating spiritual problems that will remain unresolved until they can repent and renounce the lie(s) they believe and exchange it for God's truth.

4. Some lies and demonic agreements are embedded so deeply within that we can't possibly begin to process them in our

waking state. For that reason, God might initiate our deliverance within a dream.

5. Some spiritual bondages can occur because of the land we live on. These kinds of oppression are more receptive to deliverance within the dream realm.

• THOUGHTS FOR REFLECTION •

1. Have you ever experienced personal deliverance from demonic bondage? What was that process like?
2. Have you ever been freed from demonic bondage as the result of a dream?
3. Are you challenged with the idea that Christians may also need deliverance ministry?
4. What makes deliverance ministry different between a nonbeliever and a Christian?
5. Why would Jesus choose to deliver people in dreams instead of when they are awake?

THIRTEEN

Nightmares and Sleep Disturbances

In chapter 10, I shared a dream where I went face-to-face with a demon called chaos. A short time later, another bizarre thing began happening to me at night. I'm sure it was more spiritual warfare coming against me from the region where I had just ministered, and I've never dealt with this kind before or since. While sound asleep at night, I would suddenly be awakened with emotions of deep and obsessive offense. This was not typical for me, and this strange sleep disturbance happened repeatedly. It was so strong that my entire mind felt hijacked and then shifted toward angry and intrusive thoughts.

We often connect the emotion of offense to be an attitude and a state of the heart, but what if it is more spiritual than that? I bring this up because the Holy Spirit gave me eyes to see into the situation. What I saw in the spirit was an actual demon behind the tormenting experience. Keep in mind that I'm not excusing an attitude of offense by blaming the devil. At the end of the day, I am responsible for my thoughts and the condition of my heart, only this situation had a lot more spiritual fuel on it.

I was keenly aware that every offense trying to get a grip on me was not even real but a twisted and false perception trying to take over my mind. Even though I could see and discern this clearly, I still went through all the feelings that came with it and had to resist it just the same. Thankfully, my battle ended after a few difficult months, but it taught me about the spiritual nature of offense and the importance of keeping my heart clean.

Would this be categorized as a nightmare or night terror? I'm not totally sure, but it only happened at night. I didn't have this problem during the day. God designed us to sleep well and to potentially have mighty conversations and encounters with Him while we dream at night. Our enemy Satan seems intent on creating a completely opposite experience, disturbing our sleep and traumatizing us with nightmares and night terrors.

What Are Nightmares?

I began searching the internet to find a solid definition for nightmares and most appeared to have come from the medical and psychiatric community. As expected, they emphasized the psychological and ignored the spiritual and then inferred a need for medicine if you have too many nightmares and can't sleep. One such definition states, "Nightmares are vividly realistic, disturbing dreams that rattle you awake from a deep sleep. They often set your heart pounding from fear."[1]

Some have blamed nightmares on a late-night greasy snack or their medication, but no matter what may have caused the nightmare, they are clearly the manifestation of a spirit of fear.[2] We read that "for God has not given us a spirit of fear, but of power and of love and of a sound mind" (2 Timothy 1:7). Fear is a spirit, and when it comes to nightmares and even night terrors, a spirit of fear is definitely at work. According to the Mayo Clinic, *sleep terrors*, also known as *night terrors*, are "episodes of screaming, intense fear and flailing while still asleep. Also known as night terrors, sleep terrors often are paired with sleepwalking. Like sleepwalking, sleep terrors are considered a parasomnia—an undesired occurrence during sleep. A sleep terror episode usually lasts from seconds to a few minutes, but episodes may last longer."[3] Nightmares and night terrors are then more of a spiritual problem that needs a spiritual solution to be resolved.

Some have been able to overcome persistent nightmares through targeted prayer and by playing Christian worship music while they slept. For others, much darker experiences are happening to them at night that may require inner healing and deliverance. For example, I've experienced terrible nightmares off and on for a large portion of my life, although the frequency and intensity have lessened over time. This is mostly because I'm a severe complex-trauma survivor with extreme trauma-induced amnesia. Basically, what I couldn't bring myself to remember or resolve during my waking day was showing up as violent nightmares at night.

For complex-trauma survivors, the open doors in the soul give access to spirits of fear. These open doors are far more complex. The entangled root system of complex trauma is spiritual, emotional, and physical all at the same time. This requires inner healing and deliverance ministry and, typically, a skilled Christian trauma therapist to resolve.

If this is you, I want to assure you that healing from the worst of the worst is possible as long as you are willing to do the work. I also want to encourage you to read my book *Inner Healing and Deliverance Handbook*, which navigates the complicated journey of healing from complex trauma. As you engage your healing plan, you will eventually see progress in your dreams at night. Nightmares will diminish in their frequency and intensity. Spirits of fear will lose access to your night seasons as the doors of your soul are bolted shut through healing and wholeness.

There is another kind of nightmare that people hate to discuss. It is caused by incubus and succubus spirits, and these dreams are extremely perverse in nature. Afflicted individuals usually feel too ashamed to talk about these. These spirits of the night can become very binding in the life of an individual when not dealt with, as they can interfere with a person's ability to get married or stay married and their ability to have children and can even cut their life short.

Defeating Incubus and Succubus Spirits

A married woman who attended a church in our region was having a problem. She was being attacked by a demon at night. The spirit would hold her down inside her dreams and rape her, and she would wake up with scratches and bruises. When she finally told her husband, he couldn't wrap his mind around it. He thought she was experiencing a really bizarre nightmare or maybe she was having a breakdown. He changed his mind when the spirit began to attack him in the night too, and they both ended up needing intervention. What's strange is they both died prematurely, she first.

If you look at the etymology of the word *nightmare*, it does provide clues as to how people experienced nightmares centuries ago.

> "An evil female spirit afflicting men (or horses) in their sleep with a feeling of suffocation," compounded from night + mare (n.3) "a goblin that causes nightmares, incubus." . . . An 11th century gloss gives, for Latin Echo, Anglo-Saxon wudumær, a "wood-mere." In the Anglo-Saxon superstitions, the Echo was supposed to be a spirit which dwelt in the wilds and mocked people who passed there, as the nightmare tormented people in bed. [Wording slightly modified for clarity.][4]

People have asked me repeatedly to teach or write about incubus and succubus spirits, as there is so much misinformation and sensationalism surrounding the topic. I had never thought too much about it until it came to my attention one Sunday during a church service. Two people had approached me, one after the other, and both were seeking deliverance prayer from sexual spirits in their dreams at night. Sexual sin coupled with the occult opened the door for these spirits to afflict them, and neither person could break free of them. I began dialoguing with one of our Freedom Ministries leaders at Harvest Church to find out the frequency and cause of this kind of bondage at night. She informed me that this was a persistent issue in people requesting inner healing and deliverance ministry, and sexual sin or sexual assault was typically the root cause.

What are these spirits? A succubus spirit will come to men in the form of a nightmare. This spirit usually has sex with men in their sleep in the form of other people, usually a woman. An incubus spirit is one that has sex with women while they dream at night, and they usually take on the form of a man. The secular definition of this spirit is sex demons or night demons.[5] "These spirits victimize some people repeatedly," said Dr. Rob Reimer in his book *Soul Care*. "These people wake up in the night because it feels like someone is raping them, but no one is there. They feel all the physical sensations of sexual assault, but a demonic spirit perpetrates it."[6]

Finally, these spirits might come to a person in the dream realm and attach themselves as a spirit husband or spirit wife, even ceremoniously. Every deliverance minister that I've known who has written about this phenomenon claims it is one of the strongest bondages they've ever encountered. These spirit husbands and spirit wives will either not allow the person to be married or will harass their marriage partner and even supernaturally interfere with conception. They might also attempt to put the person or their spouse to death out of jealousy.

If you are a believer in Jesus, you have the blood of Christ and the power of the Holy Spirit. You do not have to settle for this bondage, but you'll certainly need to deal with it at the root. Some of you will need to go through the process of healing from being raped and/or being molested. If this is you, I assure you that you can heal from the worst of the worst if you are willing to do the work.

Others will need to deal with any roots or habits of perversion. The Bible says not to have even a hint of sexual immorality or impurity about you, which means you'll need to do whatever it takes to walk free from sexual addiction. (See Ephesians 5:3.) Once you've healed and shut the demonic doors to perversion, these demons no longer have points of access to come and afflict you. You can break your covenant with a spirit spouse and command it to go in Jesus's name. Given the strength of this bondage, you will most likely need help from a skilled deliverance minister.

I was speaking at a conference in Tennessee and noticed a spiritual problem attached to one of the musicians. The Holy Spirit enabled me to see a large steel collar and chain around his neck. I could not discern why it was there, but another minister addressed it with more clarity. "You are being visited in your dreams at night by a woman," he said. "The Holy Spirit has told me her name. Her name is Nyra!" When he revealed the spirit's name, the man fell to the ground, shaking with loud groans. He was being delivered from a spirit wife that had taken him over in the night. By the power of the Holy Spirit, this terrible chain was broken, and he was set free.

Night-Watch Prayer Provides a Covering

Without a proper prayer shield, demonic spirits can run wild in your dreams at night. As I explained earlier, they will try to plant seeds of sinister plans into your heart in order to derail your life. They will attempt to chain you with hard bondage, terrify you, rob you of sleep, and do whatever they can do to take control of your night seasons.

One ministry wife was having a strong battle with her emotions during a pregnancy. When I began to share about the realm of dreams and what both God and Satan are doing at night, she instantly recognized the source of her emotional distress. "During the day, I'm living out what I'm dreaming at night," she explained. "I didn't see the connection until now." I prayed some fierce prayers over her night seasons, that she would win the battle for her dreams and emerge victorious in her emotions. I also counseled her to set up a regular night-watch prayer at her church and the need to raise the prayer shield at night. Her problem was a spiritual problem, and it needed a spiritual solution.

Every church should have a set time to come together for prayer and intercession. That can happen at any time during the day or week and also during the night. The prophet Isaiah described the modern church as a house of prayer for all nations. (See Isaiah 56:7.) A strong and vibrant church, then, will be a church that knows how to pray and regularly comes together for prayer. One of the benefits of a praying church is that it raises a spiritual hedge around the church and the city. We read, "And seek the peace of the city where I have caused you to be carried away captive, and pray to the LORD for it; for in its peace you will have peace" (Jeremiah 29:7).

Night-watch prayer, or praying through the night, is a form of watchman prayer, which involves a protective and defensive kind of prayer. We learn about this from the prophet Ezekiel, who was called a watchman for Israel by the Lord, and his function was to watch, pray, and warn. (See Ezekiel 3:17.)

Night-watch prayer is also quite historical. Most Christians today don't realize that observing regular watches for prayer was considered a normal part of the Christian life in the first few centuries. These prayer watches were designed to maintain the practice of offering God a "continual sacrifice of praise and prayer." They've evolved into one of the ways we act continuously as a house of prayer for all nations and watch in prayer for the return of the Lord. We read, "Watch therefore, for you know neither the day nor the hour in which the Son of Man is coming" (Matthew 25:13).

What does it mean to watch? The word translated *watch* means to have the alertness of a guard at night. Understand that a night watchman has to be more vigilant than a daytime guard. During the daytime, danger can more easily be spotted from a distance. However, everything is different at night. A night watchman must use all their senses—not just sight—to detect danger. He or she is often alone in the darkness with fewer defenses at hand. There may be no indication of enemy attack until it actually happens, so he or she must be hypervigilant and expecting danger at any moment. Jesus spoke about this type of watching.[7]

My fiercest seasons of spiritual warfare happened as the result of demonic dreams that I had at night. These dreams all happened during seasons when we, as a church, did not have night-watch prayer. For this reason, I've personally learned and taught the necessity of night-watch prayer as a covering and shield for the realm of dreams, among other things. We read, "Watch therefore, for you do not know when the master of the house is coming—in the evening, at midnight, at the crowing of the rooster, or in the morning" (Mark 13:35). This verse gives us some direction as to some watch points: in the evening, at midnight, at the crowing of the rooster, and in the morning.

In his book *Reordering Your Day*, Chuck Pierce describes specific breakthroughs and specific prophetic promises that you can enter, depending on what time you watch in prayer. Here is a summary of what he wrote:

1. Evening watch: 6:00 p.m. to 9:00 p.m.—Pray this watch for the establishing of right relationships, for a change of seasons, and to recover your losses (Genesis 24:63; Matthew 14:15–23; Genesis 8:11; 1 Samuel 30:17).

2. Midnight watch: 9:00 p.m. to 12:00 a.m.—This watch is a time for thanksgiving, for heavenly visitation, for divinely directed change, for breakthrough, and for a release of heavenly strategy (Acts 16:25–26; 27:27; Luke 11:5).

3. Breaking of a day (cock-crowing) watch: 12:00 a.m. to 3:00 a.m.—This is a watch to break the spirit of unbelief and to establish the direction of your path. It also is a watch to deal with a covenant-breaking spirit (Mark 13:35; Matthew 26:34, 74).

4. Morning watch: 3:00 a.m. to 6:00 a.m.—This watch is aligned to the morning light and the changing from darkness to light. It's a watch to awaken spiritual ears to hear the Lord and to awaken joy (Exodus 14:24; 34:2; Psalm 30:5; Isaiah 50:4).[8]

My church and I have had years of experience with night-watch prayer. We've discovered that prayer at night releases divine encounters and heavenly breakthroughs. People will receive dreams that lead them to salvation and also dreams that bring deliverance, healing, and financial breakthroughs. A huge benefit of night-watch prayer is that it shields and covers the realm of dreams at night both personally and for the church and city. This is important because without a shield, people of all ages get demonically hijacked in their dreams and wake up mentally afflicted, addicted, possessed, perverted, and more. Personally, I haven't suffered nearly the warfare in my dreams at night since we've instituted regular times of night-watch prayer.

How, then, do you know which watch is for you? Many people find themselves waking up at night during a set time, such as 2:00 a.m. or 3:33 a.m. or something else. I've always counseled people that your watch is most likely the time at night that you consistently find yourself already awake. Instead of going back to sleep, take some time to pray. You've been awakened for a purpose.

This Is for a Good Night's Sleep

Are you struggling to sleep at night? Do you have nightmares, night terrors, or other sleep disturbances? Just to reiterate, the realm of dreams is highly contested because of how powerful it is to your future. The divinely inspired contents of your dreams are also an utter upset to demonic powers. I've been in several conferences where multitudes of people have needed and received deliverance from demons that were invading their dreams or severely impacting their ability to sleep. Either way, we've been given a sure promise, and we can stand on it. We read, "He gives His beloved sleep" (Psalm 127:2), and "When you lie down, you will not be afraid; yes, you will lie down and your sleep will be sweet" (Proverbs 3:24). Sleep is a gift from God Himself, and my prayer is that He give this to you now.

1. I command your healing and deliverance from root causes of sleep disorders.
2. I command your deliverance from night terrors and insanity.
3. I reverse every assignment deposited in you by Satan in the night through your dreams.
4. I speak deliverance over you from suicidal thoughts that strike at night.
5. I speak deliverance from addictions that began in dreams at night.

6. I speak deliverance from perversions that began in dreams at night.

7. I ask for dreams to be sent that result in salvation.

8. I cover your night seasons and your dreams with the blood of Jesus.

9. I release inventions and business ideas in the night.

10. I ask for revelation of God's deep things that are "in the dark"—Job 12:22; Daniel 2:22.

11. I ask for the release of God's instructions at night.

12. I command your eyes to see into the night visions and for wisdom in what you see.

• KINGDOM PRINCIPLES •

1. God designed us to sleep well and to have mighty conversations and encounters with Him while we dream at night. Our enemy Satan seems intent on creating a completely opposite experience, disturbing our sleep at night and traumatizing us with nightmares and night terrors.

2. Some have blamed nightmares on a late-night greasy snack or on medication, but no matter what may have caused the conditions for a nightmare, I believe they are clearly the manifestation of a spirit of fear (2 Timothy 1:7).

3. Persistent nightmares are a spiritual problem that needs a spiritual solution. Some overcome these battles through targeted prayer and by playing Christian worship music while they sleep. Others deal with much darker experiences happening to them at night that may require inner healing and deliverance.

4. Another kind of nightmare that people hate to discuss is caused by incubus and succubus spirits. These dreams are very perverse in nature. Those who are afflicted by these dreams usually feel too ashamed to talk about them.

5. Night-watch prayer, or praying through the night, is a form of watchman prayer, which involves a protective and defensive kind of prayer. Prayer at night raises the shield against nightmares and releases divine encounters and heavenly breakthroughs.

• THOUGHTS FOR REFLECTION •

1. Have you ever struggled with nightmares? If so, were you able to resolve them?

2. Why might someone need inner healing and deliverance ministry to get relief from persistent nightmares?

3. Should you attempt a medicinal approach to shutting down nightmares? Why or why not?

4. Have you ever been afflicted with incubus or succubus spirits at night? If so, how strongly? Have you sought help from a deliverance counselor?

5. Do you participate in night-watch prayer? If so, what is your prayer shift at night?

Common Dream Elements and What They Mean

I've heard and read thousands of different dreams and have noticed certain dream elements are common to most people and often with a similar meaning: having babies, dying, flying, losing your teeth, running laboriously slow, losing your wallet, and more. Have you ever had one or more of these kinds of dreams? I've listed some common dream elements below along with a short, generalized meaning to help you accelerate your interpretative process.

1. Babies, pregnant, giving birth

Most of the time, this kind of dream is symbolic. Men and women can both have this kind of dream because of its metaphorical meaning. When you dream about babies, being pregnant, or having a baby, it's typically pointing to something new being birthed in your life. This could be a new relationship, a new job or church, a new ministry or anointing, coming up with a new invention or creative idea, etc. Sometimes this dream is revealing a need for spiritual maturity in one way or another (see 1 Corinthians 3:1 and Hebrews 5:13).

2. Being chased

Being chased in a dream is very intense most of the time and can be very frightening. Sometimes, you will have this dream when there is an evil spirit at work to hinder your life and delay your progress. If this is the case, you'll need to take authority over that spirit and command it to go in Jesus's name. Another reason you might have a dream about being chased is because your unfulfilled destiny in God is trying to get your attention. It's time to fulfill it, and your future is chasing you down inside your dream to get your attention.

3. Cars or vehicles

Different vehicles have different meanings. Was it a car, boat, bicycle, bus, or plane? If you dreamed you were driving a car, for example, the context and what kind of car matters. Was it a luxury car, sports car, convertible, or an old beat-up car? If you dream you are in a sports car, for example, it could mean you are receiving power to move fast and easily navigate quick turns in life. You can't take many people with you in a sports car, however, which makes the dream more about you and getting somewhere fast. This is quite different than driving a van in a dream. You can take more people in a van, only you might not go as fast. If you are driving a jeep or a vehicle made for rugged terrain, that's exactly what it implies. You are being given the ability to handle rough roads and will take paths that other people are not equipped to take. Driving a low-sitting vehicle versus a high-sitting vehicle suggests where your perspective might be. Also, if you are the driver versus the passenger, this indicates who is leading the journey. Now what if you dream about being on a bus? Is it a school bus? That indicates a journey that involves learning. If you dream about riding a bicycle or motorcycle, these are about something you are doing or will be doing as an individual. One indicates that you are doing all the labor, and the other, that you are being empowered to move quickly through obstacles and up steep terrain if needed. If you dream about being in an airplane, that is usually a good dream. You are going high, fast, and with power, and you are also going with a lot of people.

4. Deceased relatives

Sometimes God will get His message across to you but through a symbolic person (e.g., a parent or a favorite grandparent), one you would most likely hear from and listen to if they were still alive. Other times, especially if you are still grieving their death, you might dream about them as part of your grieving process. We sometimes work through grief this way. We simply dream it out and process it. Finally, and depending on the context, the dream might be pointing to either a generational curse that needs to be broken or a generational blessing that needs to be picked up.

5. Dying

Most of the time, dreaming about your own death is about a change and not an actual premonition that you will die soon. This kind of dream might be pointing to a coming change to your behavior, such as a tendency toward rage, overeating, lasciviousness, laziness, etc. Something in your flesh is going to die and needs to. It could also be pointing to a change of season that God is preparing you for, such as a change in your employment or in a relationship.

6. Falling

This can be either a positive or negative dream, although it feels absolutely terrible, in my opinion. In a positive sense, the Lord could be instructing you to let go of something and trust Him to catch you. If you fall and then wake up with a jolt, the Holy Spirit might be waking you up to something new. In a negative sense, your life could be falling out of control and even heading for a crash or failure. You'll need to pray and ask the Holy Spirit for wisdom and an appropriate action plan.

7. Flying

In these dreams, you are empowered to fly, and this is usually a good dream. Generally speaking, if you have a flying dream, then you have been given the ability to rise above something. There are also a variety of nuances when it comes to flying dreams. If you are flying low or flying high, for example, it can be an indicator of your spiritual maturity. If you are flying into outer space, you are going to have higher spiritual experiences. Sometimes in your dream, you are trying to fly but can't get off the ground, or once you become airborne, you can't control your flight too well. These are indicators that you need strength or balance if you want to rise higher in an area of your life.

8. Houses

Have you ever had a dream about a house, either your house, another house, or perhaps your childhood home? Symbolically, a house represents where you live and an aspect of your life. The context of the dream will determine its meaning. For example, if you dream about moving to a new house, that probably is about some kind of coming change: an actual physical move of some sort or an upcoming significant personal change. Different rooms in the house mean different things as well. If you dream you are on the front porch, it might be pointing to something in your future. If you dream you are on the back porch, it might be pointing to something in your past. Dreaming about your childhood home may also indicate something in your past that needs resolution.

9. Losing your cell phone, ID, wallet, or purse

Have you ever had a dream like this? When we dream about losing one of these items—a wallet, our identification, our cell phone, or our purse—it usually is pointing to losing our identity or our purpose and sense of calling. We might not know who we really are in Christ, or we might be losing aspects of our identity for a particular reason. Through this dream, God is giving us a heads-up that we need to be intentional to reorient ourselves to our God-given identity in Him.

10. Lost, late, unprepared

These kinds of dreams are a warning that you need clearer direction for your life and to seek the Lord's preparation for what is ahead of you. If you dream that you are late, you're being instructed to pay attention and not miss out on what is coming your way.

11. Running extremely slowly

Most of us have had this dream, and it's a frustrating one. When you dream that you are running extremely slowly and laboriously, this means that something is in your way: some kind of hindrance or delay, either naturally or spiritually. You will want to identify what that is so you can work through it.

12. Snakes

Many people dream about snakes, and this is usually negative. The symbolism goes back to Genesis 3 where Satan posed as a snake in the garden of Eden. He also lied and deceived God's first man and woman and thus cheated them out of their authority over the earth. Jesus described Satan as a liar and the father of all lies in John 8:44. A dream about snakes typically has something to do with a lie at work in your life. A lie is trying to attach itself to you, or you believe a lie that is harming you. God sees what we really believe in our hearts and knows when we believe the truth or a lie. He's awakening you in the night to a need for His truth and clarity by giving you this kind of dream. It is a holy alert to begin searching out the lie with the help of the Holy Spirit so you can make the necessary internal adjustments.

13. Taking a test

When you dream that you are taking a test, it's typically about some kind of preparation. You are being prepared for some kind of advancement or promotion, and the context will tell you more about that. Did you pass the test in the dream? Did you feel prepared to take the test? Were you late or early to the test? These little details will all have meaning for the final interpretation of your dream.

14. Teeth falling out

A lot of people dream that their teeth are falling out. To better understand this symbol in your dream, think about what teeth do. They chew on something so your body can process and digest it. The Word of God is spiritual food, and we chew on it by thinking and meditating on it so we can understand it and get advice and direction from it. When your teeth are falling out, it usually means that you are missing something, not understanding something, in need of wisdom, or something is off and out of place. We can also better understand this kind of dream by taking note of which teeth are falling out. If your wisdom teeth fall out, that's a very clear metaphor that you need wisdom in a particular area of your life. If your front teeth fall out or break, you are taking on more than you can handle. If it's your eye teeth, you probably need to see something with more clarity. If you dream that your baby teeth have fallen out, this means you are in transition from immaturity to maturity, which is a good dream, in my opinion. If you dream that your teeth are rotting, something corrosive or dangerously unhealthy is happening and needs attention.

15. Using the bathroom or toilet

The bathroom and toilet represent a place to get clean or to detox. You are going to get rid of something, either something light and easy or very deep. If you dream you are using a toilet in public, it means you're letting something go or something needs to get cleaned up in your life. The reason for the public viewing is about your ability to be open and vulnerable about your problems. If parts of the bathroom—the toilet, shower, sink, etc.—are dirty, this probably means you have something you need to work through and detox from, but you haven't found the right help yet so that can happen. If something in your dream smells like a dirty bathroom, again this is something that needs attention and needs to be purified. If there is a clog in the bathroom, that probably means you are holding on to something negative, usually unforgiveness. If you dream about needing to use the bathroom before you go somewhere, this means you need to clean up something in your life before you can move forward.

Deliverance Prayers from the Python Spirit

"It happened that as we were going to the place of prayer, a slave woman who had a spirit of divination met us, who was bringing great profit to her masters by fortune-telling." (Acts 16:16 NASB). The spirit of divination referred to in this verse is actually a python spirit and historically believed to be the guardian spirit for the oracle of Delphi.[1] Think of how the python behaves in the natural, and you will understand how the spirit manifests in people, even those who believe in Jesus but are unaware of it.

This spirit does a lot of evil things, but a few characteristics of this kind of attack against you is to squeeze the life out of you, suffocate you, constrict you, confine you, and to tightly restrict you into a maddening frustration. Many people with chronic breathing issues are not dealing with a physical issue as much as they are dealing with a spiritual issue. It fiercely attacks both prayer and the gift of prophecy, both of which are the antithesis of a python spirit because they breathe the life of God into people and places. This is why the slave girl interrupted Paul and his companions on their way to prayer.

With that said, if you or someone you know is struggling to breathe and has persistent respiratory issues, let's pray into this together and stand on some Bible promises:

1. Repent, renounce (means to divorce), and cast out the spirit of divination and generational divination:[2]
   - In the name of Jesus, I repent of any and all involvement with divination, either knowingly or unknowingly, in my life or in my family line. I renounce the spirit of divination and command it to leave me now. Jesus, cover me with your blood, and Holy Spirit, come and fill every place that divination had a hold on me.
2. Pray to restore the breath:
   - Breathe into my nostrils the breath of life (Genesis 2:7).
   - I will never turn my back on you: breathe life into my lungs so I can shout your name! (Psalm 80:18 MSG).
   - I bless God every chance I get; my lungs expand with His praise (Psalm 34:1).
3. Pray to release prayer and the prophetic:
   - Jesus said, "When you pray . . . " and so I will pray (Matthew 6:5).
   - We are a house of prayer (Matthew 21:13).
   - The Spirit of God has been poured out on me. I will prophesy, have visions, and dream dreams (Acts 2:17).
   - I desire to prophesy. I have faith to prophesy. We can all prophesy (1 Corinthians 14:1; Romans 12:6; 1 Corinthians 14:31).
4. Pray to receive the mind of Christ and to overturn python thinking, which is constricted, restricted thinking:
   - I am invited into God's thoughts and I am invited into God's ways (Isaiah 55:8).
   - I have the mind of Christ (1 Corinthians 2:16).
   - I will not be reduced. I will only increase, based on the story of Hannah in 1 Samuel.
   - The Lord will increase me and my children more and more (Psalm 115:14).

Appendix 3

Deliverance Prayers from the Spirit of Fear[1]

"For God has not given us a spirit of fear, but of power and of love and of a sound mind" (2 Timothy 1:7). If you are wondering if fear is an overwhelming emotion or if it has spiritual dimensions, consider that there are more than five hundred categorized phobias, ranging from claustrophobia (the fear of confined spaces) to nyctophobia (the fear of the dark).[2] Phobias, panic attacks, nightmares, night terrors, and similar fear-based issues are all rooted in the spirit of fear. You have to combat fear with faith. Here are some faith statements that have been adapted from *The Inner Healing and Deliverance Handbook* to help you overcome fear:

- In Jesus's name, I repent of and renounce every spirit of fear and every spirit that has afflicted me through the doorway of fear. I command the fear of sickness, plague, disease, and infirmity to go. The fear of dying and premature death and destruction must leave me now.
- I refuse the fear of lack, poverty, joblessness, not succeeding, not prospering, not having enough, lost business and

lost income. I repent of the fear of the unknown and having an uncertain future right now. I will not fear!

- I repent of and renounce spirits of depression, weariness, sadness, isolation, loneliness, hopelessness, despondency, despair, and discouragement.
- I repent of and renounce spirits of anger, frustration, rage, violence, and abuse. I refuse all spirits of grief, hurt, and despair over lost loved ones.
- I repent of and renounce all spirits of alcohol, drug addiction, and any addictions in Jesus's name.
- I command spirits of stress, worry, anxiety, confusion in the mind, mental breakdown, insanity, nervousness, and panic attacks to go. I have a sound mind!
- I command every spirit of hell released through bad news and bad-news reports to leave and never return.
- I command spirits of unbelief, doubt, backsliding, and lost intimacy with God to go. In Jesus's name, I bind and forbid the strongman and the ruling spirit of this nation from afflicting me with fear in any way.
- Thank You, Jesus, for abundant life, long life, and Psalm 91 life and for delivering me from every fear assignment from hell. Thank You for Your joy, peace, health, favor, abundant prosperity, and a good night's sleep. *Amen!*

Notes

Introduction

1. Jennifer Eivaz, *Glory Carriers* (Minneapolis: Chosen Books, 2019), 81–86.

2. The Bible refers to Leviathan in Psalms, Isaiah, and the book of Job. A lengthy description is found in Job 41: "Can you draw out Leviathan with a hook, or snare his tongue with a line which you lower?" (v. 1) and ends with "He beholds every high thing; he is king over all the children of pride" (v. 34).

3. As I said in *Glory Carriers*, "'It happened that as we were going to the place of prayer, a slave woman who had [was possessed with] a spirit of divination met us, who was bringing great profit to her masters by fortune-telling' (Acts 16:16 NASB). The spirit of divination referred to in this verse is actually a python spirit and historically believed to be the guardian spirit for the oracle of Delphi. Think of how a python spirit behaves in the natural, and you will get the picture." (81–82).

4. "Aboriginal Dreamtime," Artlandish Aboriginal Art Gallery, accessed June 27, 2023, https://www.aboriginal-art-australia.com/aboriginal-art-library/aboriginal-dreamtime/; Pastor Jennifer Kennedy from the aboriginal Indigenous Gamilaraay tribe, Sydney, Australia; "Aboriginal People," Survival International, accessed June 27, 2023, https://www.survivalinternational.org/tribes/aboriginals.

5. This is a touchy subject because people often confuse it with astral projection. Those who practice astral projection actually activate their human spirit to go various places for their own purposes and without the Holy Spirit's permission. As such, astral projection is a form of sorcery and is therefore condemned by God. When your entire being or just your spirit is caught away in this manner by the Holy Spirit, you have no control of it, and it's for His purposes.

6. Wikipedia, s.v. "2019–20 Australian Brushfire Season," last modified May 25, 2023, 04:07, https://en.wikipedia.org/wiki/2019-20_Australian_bushfire_season.

Chapter 1 Awaken Your Dreams at Night

1. Paul Goodman, "The 8 Main Reasons for War," Owlcation, October 14, 2022, https://owlcation.com/social-sciences/The-Main-Reasons-For-War.

2. "A prophetic act is an act of intercession given to you by the Holy Spirit that becomes a sign and a decree to the spirit realm. God starts it, but you act on it, creating the heaven-to-earth connection." Jennifer Eivaz, *The Intercessors Handbook* (Minneapolis: Chosen Books, 2016), 103.

3. "What Are Hypnagogic Hallucinations?" WebMD, June 2, 2021, https://www.webmd.com/sleep-disorders/what-are-hypnagogic-hallucinations.

Chapter 2 Dreams Need an Interpreter

1. Jessie Szalay and Minday Weisberger, "Black widow spiders: Facts about this infamous group of arachnids," LiveScience, December 7, 2021, https://www.livescience.com/39919-black-widow-spiders.html.

2. Jennifer Eivaz, *The Intercessors Handbook* (Minneapolis: Chosen Books, 2016), 171–74.

3. James W. Goll, "Understanding Your Dreams Is Rooted in Hebraic History," God Encounters Ministry, accessed May 12, 2023, https://godencounters.com/understanding-your-dreams-is-rooted-in-hebraic-history/.

4. "What Is a Cupbearer?" Got Questions, accessed June 27, 2023, https://www.gotquestions.org/what-is-a-cupbearer.html.

5. "More Than Dreams: Muslims Coming to Christ through Dreams and Visions," Lausanne World Pulse Archives, January 2007, https://lausanneworldpulse.com/perspectives-php/595/01-2007.

6. Nicola Menzie, "Report: ISIS Fighter Who 'Enjoyed' Killing Christians Wants to Follow Jesus After Dreaming of Man in White Who Told Him 'You Are Killing My People,'" The Christian Post, June 3, 2015, https://www.christianpost.com/news/report-isis-fighter-who-enjoyed-killing-christians-wants-to-follow-jesus-after-dreaming-of-man-in-white-who-told-him-you-are-killing-my-people-139880/.

7. "Shiite Muslim Dreams of Jesus, Shares Christ Through Facebook," The Voice of the Martyrs, January 1, 2019, https://www.persecution.com/stories/shiite-muslim-dreams-of-jesus-shares-christ-through-facebook/.

8. Britannica, s.v. "hadith," accessed June 27, 2023, https://www.britannica.com/topic/Hadith.

9. Nabeel Qureshi, *Seeking Allah, Finding Jesus: A Devout Muslim Encounters Christianity* (Grand Rapids, Michigan: Zondervan, 2014), 65.

10. "What is a parable?" Got Questions, accessed June 27, 2023, https://www.gotquestions.org/what-is-a-parable.html.

11. "What is cessationism? What do cessationists believe? Is cessationism biblical?" Compelling Truth, accessed June 27, 2023, https://www.compellingtruth.org/cessationism.html.

12. Doug Addison, *Understand Your Dreams Now: Spiritual Dream Interpretation,* (Santa Maria, California: InLight Connection, 2013), Chapter 3, Kindle.

13. John Paul Jackson, *The Biblical Model of Dream Interpretation* (Lewisville, Texas: Streams Ministries International, December 1, 2006), Audio Disc 1.

Chapter 3 God Deposits His Plans in Our Dreams

1. Ryan Boykin, "The Great Recession's Impact on the Housing Market," Investopedia, November 29, 2022, https://www.investopedia.com/investing/great-recessions-impact-housing-market/; "The Subprime Mortgage Crisis: Causes and Lessons Learned," Law Shelf Educational Media, accessed June 27, 2023, https://lawshelf.com/videocoursesmoduleview/the-subprime-mortgage-crisis-causes-and-lessons-learned-module-4-of-5; The Investopedia Team, "2008 Recession: What it Was and What Caused it," Investopedia, February 7, 2023, https://www.investopedia.com/terms/g/great-recession.asp.

2. "Founder's Memorial," Kenneth Hagin Ministries, accessed August 1, 2023, https://www.rhema.org/index.php?option=com_content&view=article&id=8&Itemid=13.

Chapter 4 Who Is the Dream About?

1. Jennifer Eivaz, *Seeing the Supernatural* (Minneapolis: Chosen Books, 2017), 121.

2. Infertility is a very sensitive issue. We've learned that telling a dream about pregnancy is usually more hurtful than helpful to the person. Unless you have a strong track record for literal dream accuracy, it's probably better to write down and date this kind of dream and then share it later once they've announced their good news.

3. " Strong's G3358 – metron," Blue Letter Bible, accessed June 27, 2023, https://www.blueletterbible.org/lexicon/g3358/kjv/tr/0-1/.

Chapter 5 Is it a Good or Bad Dream?

1. "The Jewish Calendar," Calendars Throughout the Ages, accessed June 27, 2023, https://www.webexhibits.org/calendars/calendar-jewish.html.

2. Wikipedia, s.v. "*Déjà vu*," last modified June 13, 2023, https://en.wikipedia.org/wiki/Déjà_vu.

Chapter 7 You'll Connect to the Spiritual Realm in Dreams

1. "The New Age movement united a body of diverse believers with two simple ideas. First, it predicted that a New Age of heightened spiritual consciousness and international peace would arrive and bring an end to racism, poverty, sickness, hunger, and war. This social transformation would result from the massive spiritual awakening of the general population during the next generation. Second, individuals could obtain a foretaste of the New Age through their own spiritual transformation. . . . Traditional occult practices (e.g., tarot reading, astrology, yoga, meditation techniques, and mediumship) were integrated into the movement as tools to assist personal transformation." Brittanica, s.v. "New Age Movement," accessed June 27, 2023, https://www.britannica.com/topic/New-Age-movement.

2. Oxford Learner's Dictionaries, s.v. "portal (*n.*)," accessed June 27, 2023, https://www.oxfordlearnersdictionaries.com/us/definition/american_english/portal.

3. Jennifer Eivaz, *The Intercessors Handbook* (Minneapolis: Chosen Books, 2016) 171–74.

4. "What are Lucid Dreams and How Can You Have Them?" Cleveland Clinic, August 10, 2021, https://health.clevelandclinic.org/what-is-lucid-dreaming-and-how-to-do-it/.

5. My understanding is that individuals who have bound themselves to each other through rituals and/or through pagan marriage rituals did it in a manner to make it virtually impossible to break the binding. The binding is deeply spiritual as well as emotional and physical. I don't recall exactly when or how I learned this information, except that it was something I had been taught in connection with my deeply occult past.

6. Barbara Herr, "The Expressive Character of Fijian Dream and Nightmare Experiences," Wiley on behalf of the American Anthropological Association, *Ethos*, 9, no. 4, Dreams (Winter, 1981), 331–52.

7. Herr, "The Expressive Character," 331–52.

Chapter 8 God Protects You through Warning Dreams

1. "Herod Archelaus was the older brother of Herod Antipas, and both were sons born to King Herod and Malthace, a Samaritan woman who was one of his ten wives." "Archelaus," BibleVerseStudy.com, accessed June 27, 2023, https://www.bibleversestudy.com/matthew/matthew2-archelaus-herod.htm.

2. The reference in Matthew 2:23 about Jesus being called a Nazarene is not found in the OT and must have been a prophetic word passed down verbally about the Christ.

Chapter 9 Powerful Intercessory Dreams

1. *Merriam-Webster*, s.v. "intercession (*n.*)," accessed June 27, 2023, https://www.merriam-webster.com/dictionary/intercession.

Chapter 10 Miracle Provision Dreams

1. Robert Morris, *The Blessed Life* (Minneapolis: Bethany House Publishers, 2019), 58.

Chapter 11 Supernatural Healing Dreams

1. Danielle Bernock, "What Are the Names of God Found in the Bible?" Christianity.com, February 16, 2023, https://www.christianity.com/wiki/god/what-are-all-the-names-of-god.html.

2. David Kovalevich, "What is the Five Fold Ministry? 5 Gifts of Jesus Christ," Flame of Fire, July 17, 2022, https://www.ffministry.com/blog/what-is-the-five-fold-ministry; Frank Dupree, "Fivefold Ministry Functions," USCAL, accessed June 27, 2023, https://www.uscal.us/article-entries/2017/2/6/fivefold-ministry-functions-by-frank-dupree.

3. Jenny Needham, "Dream Symbols: right, left, front, and back—and what they mean," Heaven's Dream Messages, accessed June 27, 2023, https://heavensdreammessages.com/2021/07/17/biblical-symbolism-right-left-front-back-in-dreams/.

4. "4982: sozo," Bible Hub, accessed June 2, 2023, https://biblehub.com/greek/4982.htm.

5. "What is Sozo?" SOZO, accessed August 3, 2023, https://bethelsozo.ch/what-is-sozo/.

Chapter 12 Dreams That Bring Deliverance

1. The Free Dictionary, s.v., "escalade," accessed June 27, 2023, https://www.thefreedictionary.com/escalade.

2. Wikipedia, s.v. "Liliana," last modified June 21, 2023, https://en.wikipedia.org/wiki/Liliana.

3. "How Trauma Affects Our Health," University of California San Francisco, accessed June 27, 2023, https://cthc.ucsf.edu/why-trauma/; Christine Richmond, "Emotional Trauma and the Mind-Body Connection," WebMD, November 29, 2018, https://www.webmd.com/mental-health/features/emotional-trauma-mind-body-connection.

Chapter 13 Nightmares and Sleep Disturbances

1. Hilary Parker, "Nightmares in Adults," WebMD, May 30, 2023, https://www.webmd.com/sleep-disorders/nightmares-in-adults.

2. I've included prayers to defeat the spirit of fear in the appendix section of the book.

3. "Sleep Terrors (Night Terrors)," Mayo Clinic, accessed June 27, 2023, https://www.mayoclinic.org/diseases-conditions/sleep-terrors/symptoms-causes/syc-20353524.

4. Online Etymology Dictionary, s.v. "nightmare (*n.*)," accessed June 27, 2023, https://www.etymonline.com/word/nightmare.

5. Kimberly Daniels, *Breaking the Power of Familiar Spirits* (Lake Mary, Florida: Charisma House, 2018), 109.

6. Rob Reimer, *Soul Care: Seven Transformational Principles for a Healthy Soul* (Franklin, Tennessee: Carpenter's Son Publishing, 2016), Kindle.

7. "What does it mean to watch and pray?" Got Questions, accessed June 27, 2023, https://www.gotquestions.org/watch-and-pray.html.

8. Chuck Pierce, *Reordering Your Day: Understanding and Embracing the Four Prayer Watches* (Denton, Texas: Glory of Zion International Ministries, 2006), 51.

Appendix 2 Deliverance Prayers from the Python Spirit

1. "Python," Bible Hub, accessed June 27, 2023, https://biblehub.com/topical/p/python.htm.

2. Word Hippo, s.v. "renounce, (*v.*)," accessed June 21, 2023, https://www.wordhippo.com/what-is/another-word-for/renounce.html.

Appendix 3 Deliverance Prayers from the Spirit of Fear

1. Adapted from Jennifer Eivaz, *The Inner Healing and Deliverance Handbook* (Minneapolis: Chosen Books, 2022), 201.

2. Rosey LaVine, "The Ultimate List of 550+ Phobias From A to Z," Science of People, accessed June 27, 2023, https://www.scienceofpeople.com/list-of-phobias/.

Jennifer Eivaz (JenniferEivaz.com) is a minister and international conference speaker with a heart to equip the church in the supernatural and to raise up passionate and effective prayer warriors. She is a content contributor for many online Christian publications, has been featured on several Christian television shows, hosts the popular podcast *Take Ten With Jenn*, and has authored several bestselling books. Jennifer and her husband, Ron, co-pastor Harvest Church, now meeting in several locations in addition to hosting a thriving online campus. They also have two wonderful children.